Household energy and the poor in the third world

ELIZABETH CECELSKI, JOY DUNKERLEY, and WILLIAM RAMSAY
with an appendix by EMMANUEL MBI

RESEARCH PAPER R-15

RESOURCES FOR THE FUTURE / WASHINGTON, D.C.

RESOURCES FOR THE FUTURE, INC.
1755 Massachusetts Avenue, N.W., Washington, D.C. 20036

Resources for the Future is a nonprofit organization for research and education in the development, conservation, and use of natural resources and the improvement of the quality of the environment. It was established in 1952 with the cooperation of the Ford Foundation. Grants for research are accepted from government and private sources only if they meet the conditions of a policy established by the Board of Directors of Resources for the Future. The policy states that RFF shall be solely responsible for the conduct of the research and free to make the research results available to the public. Part of the work of Resources for the Future is carried out by its resident staff; part is supported by grants to universities and other nonprofit organizations. Unless otherwise stated, interpretations and conclusions in RFF publications are those of the authors; the organization takes responsibility for the selection of significant subjects for study, the competence of the researchers, and their freedom of inquiry.

Research Papers are studies and conference reports published by Resources for the Future from the authors' typescripts. The accuracy of the material is the responsibility of the authors and the material is not given the usual editorial review by RFF. The Research Paper series is intended to provide inexpensive and prompt distribution of research that is likely to have a shorter shelf life or to reach a smaller audience than RFF books.

Library of Congress Catalog Card Number 79-4863
ISBN 0-8018-2283-1

Copyright © 1979 by Resources for the Future, Inc.

Manufactured in the United States of America

Published July 1979. $6.75

TABLE OF CONTENTS

PAGE

Foreword

This research paper originated in a request from the Energy, Water, and Telecommunications Department of the World Bank to Resources for the Future to conduct a preliminary study for a research project on energy needs and possibilities for the poor in developing countries. Specifically, the emphasis was to be on household energy consumption (that is, energy used for cooking, heating where appropriate, and lighting) of both the urban and rural poor, and on possibilities of supplying these needs in an improved way, particularly through new or unconventional technologies such as biogas, solar power, mini hydro, and wind, as well as the more conventional and tra-ditional wood products, petroleum products and central station electricity. A report on these issues, entitled "Household Energy Use and Supply by the Urban and Rural Poor in Developing Countries," was delivered to the World Bank in October 1978.

Within the necessarily limited scope of the project, however, it was not possible to do justice to a whole series of questions which are of direct relevance to the energy consumption of the poor, and in particular to the introduction of changes in demand or supply patterns. As research on domestic energy use shows, energy usage in both developed and developing countries is deeply embedded in established ways of thinking and behavior-- as well as not so obvious economic and institutional incentives and constraints. It is therefore difficult and perhaps unrealistic to consider changing energy usage without examining its ramifications for these other aspects of individual and commercial life. In consequence, with the aid of funds made available by the RFF Center for Energy Policy Research from a Ford Foundation research grant, we tried to deal with some of these questions--the cultural aspects of energy consumption, implications for income distribution and equity, and the institutional arrangements.

During the course of our investigation, it became clear that data on all aspects of energy consumption by the poor in developing areas as in developed, are extremely scanty and often suspect. We nonetheless felt, given the immense interest in this subject, both in this country and abroad, that it was worthwhile publishing our work at this stage, despite its preliminary nature. Moreover, the study brings together in one place information on published sources and should serve as a valuable bibliography in a field which is as yet poorly structured and whose literature is widely scattered.

Poor as the data are, they permit some broad conclusions to be drawn. First, energy is used with great inefficiency in many parts of the developing world; second, there exist great opportunities for important savings if efficiencies can be improved; and third, cultural and institutional factors are important in changing energy technologies. The authors think these broad conclusions will survive the results of further research, but emphasize that further investigation is necessary before more specific policy recommendations can be made. In the words of the authors, ". . .regardless of whether developmental objectives are oriented to the provision of cooking needs, or to rapid economic growth with or without redistribution, there is still insufficient knowledge of the energy economy patterns of the urban and rural poor to develop consistent energy programs."

Material from Chapters II and III has been presented at the Consulta del Caribe Sobre Energia y Agricultura, held from November 29 to December 1, 1978, in Santo Domingo, Dominican Republic, and the International Energy Seminar at the Administrative Staff College, held January 4-7, 1979, in

Hyderabad, India. Part of Chapter II will also be published in a forth-coming issue of the Natural Resources Forum of the United Nations.

The main body of the text was prepared by William Ramsay, Senior Fellow; Joy Dunkerley, Senior Research Associate; and Elizabeth Cecelski, Research Assistant, all of the CEPR. Emmanuel Mbi, then of CEPR, now of the World Bank, prepared the annex on Cameroon.

Hans H. Landsberg
Director
Center for Energy Policy Research

Acknowledgments

The authors wish to express their thanks to all those of the development and energy communities, too numerous to distinguish individually, who gave us the benefit of their experience and insights. We also benefitted from the comments and criticisms of RFF colleagues Lincoln Gordon, Hans Landsberg, Robert Mitchell, and Ronald Ridker. Anthony Pryor of the Rockefeller Foundation and Willian Knowland of the Overseas Development Council provided extensive comments.

Efrain Friedmann, David Hughart and Jeremy Warford of the Energy, Water and Telecommunications Department of the World Bank provided the initial idea and partial support for the study. However, views expressed are those of the authors and do not necessarily reflect those of the World Bank. The remainder of the study was financed by a grant from the Ford Foundation.

The secretaries of the RFF Center for Energy Policy Research prepared this manuscript with their customary efficiency and good humor. Special thanks are due to Loretta Burgess, our project secretary, and to Cherry Arnold-Johnson, Adrienne Plater, and Greta Sorenson in word processing.

Chapter I

INTRODUCTION AND OVERVIEW

The purpose of this research paper is to bring together what is known about household energy consumption among the poor in developing countries and supply alternatives for meeting those needs, as well as results of some limited experiments in introducing new forms of energy.

There are several reasons for investigating this topic. First, the provision of household energy needs takes up a substantial part of the resources of poor households--either in cash purchases or in the time required to gather wood or crop and animal wastes. Rising prices of oil products and, in some areas, diminishing fuel wood supplies are likely to make these problems more acute in future. Second, at the lowest income levels, energy is used almost exclusively to satisfy the most basic of human needs, in particular food preparation. Any curtailment in consumption from this already low level would lead to a decline in nutrition standards, and a concomitant decline in productive capacities.

From the public policy point of view, this topic is also of major importance. Household energy consumption accounts for a major part of total energy consumption (about 50 percent) in developing countries, and a substantial part of this share is consumed by those who can be described as poor. Second, overuse of firewood, the main fuel of the rural poor, can lead to widespread deforestation and soil erosion, and therefore reduce agricultural productivity. Furthermore, increasing demand for kerosine, widely used in towns, can put pressure on already strained foreign exchange budgets.

It can be argued that policy towards poor households might most efficiently be directed to the provision of energy in a way that will make the greatest contribution to a nation's total output, thereby raising income and employment among the poor who could then provide for their household energy needs in the way they feel best. But increasing income alone may not automatically solve this problem. Some new energy systems could initially worsen the distribution of income. And high first costs of a new system (such as an improved wood burning stove) may continue to inhibit widespread adoption even at higher income levels.

Although the special nature of household energy and the poor is widely recognized--the governments of many developing nations have long-standing subsidy programs for both kerosine and rural electricity supplies--there is a serious lack of reliable information available on the level and quality of energy services at present consumed by the poor. Furthermore, there has been little analytic study of how rapidly the energy consumption of the poor will rise in the future and how these needs will be met. The present study reviews the limited and inadequate data available and attempts to address some of the analytic issues involved.

This project is confined by hypothesis to the domestic energy services consumed by poorer households. Therefore, we deal only with meeting household energy needs, and do not address the relationship between energy consumption and economic development on an economy-wide scale. Even within the confines of our study, however, developmental concerns play an important indirect role. Thus, increases in income accompanying economic growth would lead both to rises in household energy consumption and to changes in the composition of that consumption. And a policy emphasizing the provision of basic needs (such as housing, food, water, education) would increase both the derived demand for energy as effective incomes rise, and the use of energy embodied in such services.

This report first constructs in Chapter II household energy consumption patterns of the urban and rural poor in the developing world, and then in Chapter III analyzes supply possibilities. Additional considerations on the demand side--the role of cultural preferences in energy use--and on the supply side--the importance of income distribution patterns in the implementation of new energy technologies--are then analyzed in Chapter IV in the light of the available evidence. Some relevant examples of local and national organizational change in response to energy demand and supply constraints are examined in Chapter V. A bibliography and some observations on energy use in Cameroon by Emmanuel Mbi are included in appendices.

From the rudimentary data available, it appears (see Chapter II) that energy consumption by the rural and urban poor in much of Africa and Asia amounts to about 10 GJ [1] (0.3 tce) per head per year, a quantity reckoned to be at the margin necessary for the minimum provision of food in rural areas using existing technologies. However, the range of estimates for individual cases is very large. There appears to be little difference in consumption levels between the rural and urban poor. In Africa and Asia, proportionately higher rural consumption of low efficiency non-commercial fuels may account for the lack of differences between rural and urban energy consumption despite generally higher urban incomes.

---

[1] GJ = gigajoules = 10^9 joules = 0.948 million but = 0.035 tons coal equivalent.

A further tentative conclusion is that for similar reasons, related to the changing efficiency of the fuel supply system, energy consumption measured in quantity terms rises by less than the rise in income--at lower income levels at least. As incomes rise, there is apparently a tendency to switch to more efficient user technologies in a manner analogous to the contrast in energy consumption patterns between urban and rural areas. Thus, a rising demand for energy services can be accommodated by a less than proportionate gross input. The implications of this experience are that as incomes rise and as urbanization continues, consumption of commercial fuels-- often imported--will rise sharply. This focuses attention on new methods of moderating this fuel changeover, including the use of more local fuel resources and the improvement of energy use efficiencies.

From our brief review of new supply possibilities (see Chapter III), it appears that while various new options exist for satisfying household needs, many of the newer methods cannot be fully assessed for economic feasibility without further research and testing. However, the following rough generalizations are useful in guiding further research. Of the new methods, biogas seems furthest along and assured of some practical application. Solar cookers suffer from lack of appropriateness to end uses, so sociological feasibility remains to be tested. Wind energy could provide potable water supplies for household use at reasonable cost where conditions are suitable. Small hydroelectric facilities could provide power to some rural areas at costs below that of electricity supplies by some national grids; similarly, photovoltaic cells, even under present cost conditions, could supply some valuable services such as educational television to remote areas.

For the purely traditional fuels, options involve complex ecological, institutional, and timber production as well as energy and economic problems. Furthermore, important parts of the assessment of these questions still depend on as yet incomplete demand information. However, improved stoves for both wood and charcoal fuels appear to be a least-cost tactic for a provisional tempering of fuelwood and related charcoal supply crises.

In the context of poverty, an abstract economic comparison of supply and demand is of course an incomplete analysis. Cultural and equity factors (see Chapter IV) appear particularly significant in the successful implementation of energy programs involving new energy sources aimed at meeting the basic household energy needs of the poor. Different frameworks of preferences--social, cultural, and religious--clearly affect how energy is used and the demands which a new energy source must meet.

Existing income distribution and ownership patterns also influence the benefits to the poor of new energy systems. For example, even investments that are economic in the long run may not be initially affordable to the poor. More careful attention needs to be paid to an analysis of the pros and cons from a social cost point of view of credits or subsidies that would enable the poor to utilize new energy sources, particularly in cases where a formerly "free" good would be monetarized as a result.

Finally, institutional mechanisms can be crucial in the introduction of new energy systems (see Chapter V). Experience with community energy systems and "appropriate technology" research as institutional approaches to addressing the energy demands of the poor demonstrates both the potentially great influence of these institutions in this area and the considerable obstacles to these approaches.

It must be emphasized that the foregoing analysis and conclusions are based on patchy and inadequate data, often difficult to interpret. Further insights into these important questions will require better information on a number of areas, including energy consumption patterns of the rural and urban poor; systems aspects of new supply alternatives—such as biogas, decentralized electricity, woodlots, and charcoal; possibilities for improved end use efficiencies; and equity implications of new energy systems, specifically the possible role of community systems and "appropriate" technologies.

Chapter II

HOUSEHOLD ENERGY CONSUMPTION BY

THE POOR IN DEVELOPING COUNTRIES

This chapter puts together available data in an attempt to draw a picture of existing patterns of energy consumption for both the rural and
urban poor, and to estimate how these patterns might be expected to change
as incomes rise.

A thoroughgoing analysis of the energy consumption of the poor would
need three kinds of information--the tasks which energy performs such as
cooking, heating, and lighting; the amount and type of each form of energy
used in performing each task; and the efficiency with which that task is
performed. Data currently available on energy consumption by the poor in
developing areas falls well short of the ideal in all three respects.

Energy Tasks

The form in which energy is consumed is among other factors closely
related to the tasks it is designed to perform. For the urban and rural
poor, these are habitually summed up as "cooking and lighting" of which
cooking is usually estimated to account for about 80 percent. Even such a
rudimentary breakdown is, however, misleading. Lighting may not exist as a
separate energy task for large numbers of the developing world whose working
day is geared to hours of daylight. And if artificial light is needed, it
might be provided with sources of energy which are not included here, such
as candles, vegetable oil lamps or flashlights.

On the other hand, there is also evidence of wider energy tasks at even
very low levels of income. Thus, in rural Gambia, cooking is estimated to
account for only 53 percent of wood fuel consumption rather than the 80

percent referred to above, the balance being accounted for by water
heating (36 percent), ironing (8 percent), and protection (3 percent).[1]
Once in town, ironing takes a larger proportion of wood fuel consumption,
and, what is perhaps more important, increases interest in electricity
(which simplifies ironing dramatically). In many areas of Africa and in
the Andean countries, space heating may be a major use of fuel, though often
integrated with other energy uses.[2]

Energy Consumed by the Poor

Data on the energy used to fulfill these tasks is very sketchy. A
certain amount of data on commercial fuels exists, though rarely broken
down by end use. The position with regard to noncommercial fuels is even
less satisfactory. Indeed, in the past it has been customary to exclude
them, not because their importance was unrecognized, but mainly due to lack
of information. Recently, more attention has been paid to some of the noncommercial fuels (by, for example, the Food and Agricultural Organization
with respect to forest products). While data are still sparse, it is now
generally recognized that the quantities involved are so large that to
exclude them leads to erroneous conclusions. In this report, therefore,
unless otherwise specified, energy consumption and supplies always include
noncommercial fuels.[3]

_____

[1]Keith Openshaw, "Woodfuel, a Time for Reassessment," Natural
Resources Forum (1978).

[2]See Turi Hammer Digernes, "Wood for Fuel--Energy Crisis Implying
Desertification: The case of Bora, the Sudan," mimeo, 1977. Geografisk
Institut, Universiter, Bergen, Norway. Also see P. Fleuret and A. Fleuret
"Fuelwood Use in a Peasant Community: A Tanzanian Case Study" (mimeo).

[3]On the other hand, we have excluded animate or metabolic energy from
draft animals and human beings. These sources, however, are only marginally
amenable for increased use in supplying household energy inputs of the types
considered here.

In this connection, the distinction between commercial and noncommercial fuels, though commonly accepted in the literature, is not entirely satisfactory. The identification of commercial fuels, petroleum products (particularly kerosine), coal, town gas, bottled gas, and electricity is straightforward. In these forms of fuel and power, the producer is distinct from the consumer and the products are traded in organized markets.

But some so-called "noncommercial" fuels, fuelwood and charcoal for example, are also bought and sold in organized markets, especially in urban areas. And even the more traditional types of noncommercial energy—crop and animal wastes—though typically not paid for in cash, are often paid for in kind. Nor is the collection of twigs and leaves from common forest properties entirely costless as it diverts time and energy from other activities of possibly greater actual or potential productivity—education in the case of children, and handicrafts in the case of women, the two groups which collect much of this fuel.

The distinction between "commercial" and "noncommercial" fuels is therefore very blurred. We continue to use these terms here because of their widespread acceptance. But there is need for a new terminology which reflects more realistically the spectrum of conditions under which these fuels are traded.

The major difficulty is, however, lack of data on noncommercial fuels. In many countries no estimates of noncommercial fuel use are available, and even for countries where information is available there are major problems stemming from data accuracy, definitional problems, and the choice of conversion factors used to aggregate individual forms of fuel to a comparable (heat equivalent) basis. Estimates of fuelwood consumption typically vary widely--for Bangladesh for example by a factor of ten.[4] And even if accurate fuelwood production or consumption data were available in a common measure such as cubic meters, the accurate derivation of its calorific content requires determining the type of wood, whether the wood is stacked or solid, green or dry, and how much is consumed in the form of charcoal.

Problems also exist for dung, which provides about 10 percent of total fuel consumed in India as a whole and a higher proportion in villages. Although it is not difficult to establish credible limits to the total availability of dung based on the cattle population, the actual caloric content of the dung used for fuel by households depends inter al. on the quality of the original dung collected and the amount which is returned to the fields as fertilizer. Different assumptions about any of these relationships can result in wide divergences in estimates of net energy content of dung used by households.

Furthermore, there are also a number of noncommercial fuels such as some crop residues, twigs, and leaves whose importance is impossible to measure satisfactorily except through careful investigation of energy-using habits of households, something which has rarely been done. Estimates of energy consumption for countries which use large quantities of noncommercial fuel are consequently highly approximate. It must therefore be emphasized that much of the analysis which follows is highly speculative, based on incomplete or estimated data sources which would ideally require a detailed audit of data and analysis procedures.

---

[4] Asian Development Bank and United Nations Development Program, Bangladesh Energy Study, appendix 1, volume 2, part 5 (1976) pp. 5-10, 5-11.

Energy Consumption by the Rural Poor

Table II-1 gives various estimates of domestic energy uses in LDC
rural villages.[5] Given the integration of domestic uses with agricultural uses, and the practical difficulty of separating them, there are
possibilities of wide variation in estimates stemming from definitional
differences alone. Furthermore, as the proportion of total rural energy
used in domestic as opposed to production oriented activities varies considerably from country to country, it cannot be assumed that there is a
constant margin of error when we compare our estimates among countries.

With these caveats, it appears that consumption in India, Pakistan,
Nepal, and Bangladesh is somewhat lower (at between 3 and 11 gigajoules per
capita per year)[6] in rural districts than in most of the other developing
countries listed in table II-1. In Africa, consumption of wood alone (by
far the major source of domestic fuel in the developing countries of Africa)
varies between 10 and 20 GJ per capita annually, but the aggregation of
fuelwood on a heat content basis is beset with difficulties and may lead to
an overestimations bias. Energy consumption in Latin American rural areas
appears to be substantially above that of the other regions.

_____

[5]Data on the energy consumption of the rural poor in contrast to
that of higher income groups is not generally available. The data contained
here relate mainly to average rural consumption which for many countries
will be fairly representative of rural poverty.

[6]1 gigajoule = 10^9 joules = 0.948 million btu.

Table II-1. Estimated Energy Consumption in Rural Areas

(GJ per capita)

Country	Year	Fuel-wood	Percent charcoal	Wastes	Commercial	Total
Gambia	1973	13	9	na	na	13[a]
Kenya	1960	9.5	6	na	na	9.5[a]
Sudan	1962	16	42	na	na	16[a]
Tanzania	1968	21	1	na	na	21[a]
Uganda	1979	14	na	na	na	14[a]
Upper Volta	1977	4-7	na	3.5	na	7.5-10.5
Nigeria	1975(?)	16	na	na	0.04	16
Bolivia	1975(?)	35	na	na	na	35
Mexico	1975	15	na	na	2.8	17.8
Nepal[b]	1976	7	na	1.4	na	8.4
Thailand	1970	12	40	na	na	12[a]
Bangladesh	1973	0.4	na	2.5	0.2	3.1
Pakistan	1978	3.0	na	1.5	0.2	5.4[c]
India	1970-71	6.1	na	3.3	1.8	11.2

Sources: Major sources used in building up this table in addition to country specific sources are as follows   (see Appendix table C-1 for full citation of sources and conversion methodology):

Arjun Makhijani with Alan Poole, Energy and Agriculture in the Third World, a report to the Energy Policy Project of the Ford Foundation (Cambridge, Mass., Ballinger Publishing Company, 1975).

United Nations Food and Agriculture Organization, Yearbook of Forest Products, 1976 (1966-76) (Rome, Food and Agricultural Organization, 1978).

Asian Development Bank, United National Development Program and Republic of Bangladesh, Bangaladesh Energy Study, November 1976.

D.E. Earl, Forest Energy and Economic Development (Oxford, Clarendon Press, 1975).

(continued)

Notes to table II-1 (cont.)

Note: The unit of energy used throughout this report is gigajoule (GJ) based on the standard International System. One joule represents the amount of work or energy required to accelerate a mass of two kilograms from rest to a speed of one meter per second.

$$1 \text{ GJ} = 10^9 \text{ joules} = 0.948 \text{ mn Btu} = \frac{10^6}{4.184} \text{ kcal} = \frac{1}{3.6} \text{ Mwh}$$

$$= \frac{1}{28.8} \text{ tons coal equivalent.}$$

[a]Fuelwood, including charcoal, only.

[b]Fuelwood consumption estimates for Nepal vary.

[c]Includes 0.6 unaccounted.

With regard to type of fuel, noncommercial fuels clearly predominate in rural areas. In the African countries noncommercial fuels, fuelwood (including charcoal) and forest and crop wastes, provide virtually all domestic consumption, and in India, Pakistan, and Bangladesh, noncommercial fuels account for about 90 percent of total domestic consumption.[7] Though fuelwood and crop residues are the major forms of noncommercial fuels in these countries, dung is also important, providing as much as 50 percent of total rural energy consumption in some areas.

In Africa and the subcontintent the small amounts of commercial energy used are petroleum products (particularly kerosine) and electricity. In Mexico, where consumption of commercial fuels is larger, bottled gas is also used.

Despite the policy interest and commitment of funds to rural electrification in recent years,[8] only a relatively small proportion of the rural population has electricity: 4 percent in Africa, 15 percent in Asia, and 23 percent in Latin America.

The amounts of electricity consumed in rural areas per consumer are modest (India and El Salvador 1,000 kWh per capita per annum, Ethopia 800, and Thailand 200), and from 50 to 80 percent of those amounts are used in

---

[7] For a more detailed analysis of Indian consumption cf. Kirit Parikh, Energy: "Second India Studies," (Macmillan Company of India Limited, 1976).

[8] Total cumulative investment in rural electrification by developing countries within the World Bank's area of operations was about $10,000 million by 1971, about 10 percent of total investment in the electric power sector. World Bank, Rural Electrification (Washington, D.C., World Bank, 1975).

agricultural and commercial activities.[9] The quantities flowing to

households for domestic use are therefore very small. Even when the rural

poor have access to electricity, the relatively high first cost of hookup and

subsequent high costs of supplying electricity limit use. (See Chapter IV).

Energy Consumption by the Urban Poor

The energy consumption of the urban poor[10] has received less

attention. The results of isolated surveys of various cities are given in

table II-2. In the case of India, the range of estimates for energy con-

sumption by the poor of the three major cities is much narrower than that

of the rural estimates (at about 5-6 GJ per capita annually).[11]

A recent study of energy consumption in Pakistan (Sherman, 1978),

which does not include electricity consumption, shows a lower annual per

capita consumption of all other fuels in urban areas (3.8 GJ) compared

with rural (5.4 GJ). Part of this difference may be offset by increased

electricity consumption by those households with access to electricity,

but even among rural and urban households without access to electricity,

consumption is lower in the urban areas.

---

[9]Ibid.

[10]From the point of view of energy consumption the definition of the
urban poor is more critical than that of the rural poor. In this section
only the lowest income groups of the largest cites are considered. Note
that the incomes of the lowest income groups in Latin America are higher
than the incomes of the lowest income groups in Asia and Africa.

[11]c.f. K. Parikh op. cit.

Table II-2. Energy Consumption by Urban Poor for Domestic Use (selected urban areas)

(Gigajoules per capita per annum)

	Mexico[1] City	Mexico[2] City	Delhi[4]	Delhi[5]	Bombay[4]	Bombay[5]	Pakistan[11] urban[12]	Pakistan[11] urban[13]
Wood	1.5[3]	---	1.7[6]	1.4[7]	4.8[9]	3.3[10]	2.5	2.8
Dung	---	---	1.5	0.8	---	0.1	0.4	0.7
Crop wastes	---	---	0.2	0.1	---	---	neg.	neg.
Total non-commercial	1.5	---	3.4	2.3	4.8	3.4	2.9	3.5
Kerosene	2.9	1.5	0.2	0.2	0.8	1.1	0.6	0.3
Gas	---[3]	2.6	---	---	---	0.1	na	na
Coal	---[3]	---	1.8[8]	2.2[8]	---	0.1	na	na
Electricity	0.9	2.4	neg.	0.1	---	0.1	na	na
Others	---	---	0.2	0.1	---	0.1	na	na
Total commercial	3.8	6.5	5.2	2.5	0.8	1.5	na	na
Total	5.3	6.5	5.6	4.8	5.8	4.9	na	na

Sources: For Mexico City. Urban Energy Use Patterns in Developing Countries: A Preliminary Study of Mexico City, prepared by Gordon McGranahan and Manuel Taylor, Urban and Policy Sciences, State University of New York at Stony Brook. For Delhi and Bombay, Domestic Fuels in India, National Council of Applied Economic Research, New Delhi (Bombay, Asia Publishing House, 1959). For Pakistan, "Household Use of Energy in Pakistan" by Michel M. Sherman, Division of Economic Analysis, USAID, Islamabad, Pakistan, May 1978.

[1]Monthly family expenditure of 0-1,000 1970 pesos.

[2]Monthly family expenditure of 1,001-2,500 1970 pesos.

[3]Wood includes coal.

[4]Monthly family expenditure of 1-100 rupees.

[5]Monthly family expenditure of 101-200 rupees.

[6]Of which 0.4 charcoal.

[7]Of which 0.5 charcoal.

[8]Soft coke.

[9]Charcoal 5.2.

[10]Charcoal 2.4.

[11]Excludes electricity, diesel, and LPG

[12]Assets group I which is a proxy for the lowest income group.

[13]Assets group II which is a proxy for the next lowest income group.

In the African countries, wood fuels (which include charcoal) are the main form of energy available to the urban poor. In Gambia, Sudan, and Tanzania, wood fuel consumption per head in cities is about the same as, or a little lower than, in rural areas.[12]

Estimates for Mexico City yield a level of consumption substantially below that of rural Mexican areas. But estimates in the Mexico City study are based on assumed activity levels and on analogies with U.S. consumption parameters and may not therefore be comparable with estimates of rural energy use based on direct estimates of fuel used.[13]

Although our concern in this study is with the direct domestic consumption of energy by the poor in domestic uses rather than with the total energy embodied in all their activities, an exception should be made for transport which is not only a highly energy intensive activity used heavily by the urban poor, but is also amenable to change through city planning.

---

[12] Openshaw, op. cit.

[13] c.f. Urban Energy Use Patterns in Developing Countries: A Preliminary Study of Mexico City by Gordon McGranahan and Manuel Taylor, (Urban and Policy Sciences, State University of New York at Stony Brook, 1978). This study develops a methodology based on estimates of activity levels and energy intensities associated with activity levels. The methodology has since been extended to a study of Nairobi, G. McGranahan, S. Chubb and R. Nathans of the Institute for Energy Research, State University of New York at Stony Brook and O. Mbeche of the University of Nairobi, "Patterns of Urban Household Energy Use in Developing Countries: the Case of Nairobi," (February 1979, draft). Though primarily designed as exercises in methodology the results obtained for direct household uses at least are consistent with results obtained through sample surveys carried out in other countries.

The Mexico City study gives estimates of energy embodied in transport
by the poor and other income groups (data reproduced in table II-3).
This table indicates a very modest consumption of transport energy in the
lowest income group--6 GJ compared with 24 GJ per household in direct residential use.   But it also indicates that consumption of energy in
transportation rises very steeply as incomes rise.

In contrast with the pattern of energy use in rural areas, energy
consumption in urban areas, even among the poor, is weighted more heavily
towards commercial fuels.   In urban areas of India, for example,
"commercial" fuels (mainly soft coke and electricity) account for 60 to 70
percent of consumption (by quantity)--a much higher proportion than in rural
areas.

In Mexico City the fuel supply consists essentially of commercial
fuels.   Wood and coke are used only by the lowest income group where they
account for 30 percent of the total.   Kerosine is the major fuel in this
group, accounting for one-half; electricity supplies the remainder.

Consumption of Urban and Rural Poor Compared

On the basis of this admittedly sketchy information it appears that
the per capita consumption of energy is similar or perhaps lower among the
poor in urban areas than in rural areas, or at least does not appear
to be substantially higher.   This tentative finding is at first sight
counterintuitive.   It is generally recognized that the incomes of the

Table II-3. Mexico City Income Groups Total Energy Consumption, 1976

(Btu x 10^9)

Fuel use categories	Per family energy consumption (Btu x 10^6)				
	0–1,000	1,000–2,500	2,500–5,000	5,000–10,000	10,000–more
I Food	12.5	19.0	27.0	40.8	57.8
II Transportation	5.9	27.0	68.0	145.0	223.0
III Residential uses	22.7	27.9	32.6	51.4	58.6
Cooking	10.0	9.8	10.0	10.0	10.0
Water heat	8.6	7.9	6.2	13.9	18.1
Lighting	2.0	4.3	5.4	7.6	10.0
Appliances	2.1	5.9	9.7	17.6	18.0
Heating	--	--	1.3	2.4	2.6
IV Public services	3.7	7.5	9.0	9.6	10.5
Lighting		3.4	4.2	4.2	4.2
Water pumping	0.7	1.0	1.5	1.9	2.8
Garbage collection	0.1	0.2	0.4	0.6	0.6
Schools, offices, hospitals	2.9	2.9	2.9	2.9	2.9
V Housing	3.3	13.2	19.4	26.8	33.9
Total $\approx$	48	95	158	272	382
Households x 10^3	375.4	989.7	500.5	250.3	159.3

Source: Urban Energy Use Patterns in Developing Countries: A Preliminary Study of Mexico City. Prepared by Gordon McGranhan and Manuel Taylor, Urban and Policy Sciences, State University of New York at Stony Brook, p. 54.

Note: These data apply to the consumption of energy embodied in the various fuel use categories.

urban poor are higher than those of the rural poor, and as such would be expected to lead to higher energy consumption. What may be happening is that urban higher incomes lead to an increased demand for energy services, but that the more efficient fuel supplies available in the cities permit these energy services to be satisfied with proportionately less gross energy input.[14] A second, and related, explanation of the lower consumption relative to income in urban areas is that the price of the more efficient commercial energy is higher in urban areas where opportunities for the collection of "free" fuels are minimal.

Rising Incomes and Energy Consumption

A more direct way of assessing the effect of rising incomes on total energy consumption is to analyze the energy consumption patterns of different income groups within the same area or city. This approach has the advantage of incorporating relatively similar energy price levels into the comparison.[15]

From the studies available, covering the urban poor in Mexico City, in Bombay, Delhi and Calcutta, and the rural and urban poor in Pakistan, it appears that domestic energy consumption rises much less than income, at least among the lowest income groups. In the Indian cities for example,

---

[14]The Mexico City study, for example, indicates a fourfold improvement in energy efficiencies in cooking with kerosine (more typically a city fuel) rather than wood.

[15]Prices of energy to the urban rich and poor will not be identical For kerosine, the rich, buying less often in larger quantities, probably pay somewhat lower prices than the poor who buy much of their fuel supplies from itinerant vendors at very frequent intervals. Nonetheless, the difference in prices paid is probably less between groups in a city than between city and rural areas.

energy consumption per household in quantity terms rises at about

one-third of the rate of increase in income. As household size is larger at

higher incomes in India, however, per capita consumption stays virtually

constant in the three lowest income groups, though it does rise thereafter.

Estimates given in the Mexico City study indicate a very gradual

increase in residential energy consumption per household through the

rising income groups. In all cases the rate of increase is much less than

the rise in incomes. Households with an income of less than 1,000 (1970)

pesos a month consume 24 GJ annually while households with incomes more

than ten times higher consume only two and a half as much (62 GJ).

The Pakistan study gives energy consumption by various land-holding

and asset groups as a proxy for income groups. The rise in energy con-

sumption from one group to another is moderate and probably substantially

less than the rise in income level associated with the different asset

and land-holding groups.

In the literature, the quantity of energy consumed by the poor is fre-

quently described as "inelastic" in the sense that it is a basic necessity

which must be provided under all circumstances.[16] This hypothesis of

inelasticity has two aspects. It implies first that energy consumption is

not responsive to price changes. There is little data to establish or

refute this view, although it is clearly a highly relevant topic given the

sharp rise in fuel prices which has taken place since 1973. But, second,

the data presented here appear to indicate a certain income inelasticity of

_____

[16]Note that even at the lowest levels of energy consumption, there
are possibilities of further reductions through, for example, a reduction in
the number of hot meals per day.

demand for energy or at least gross energy inputs, at low levels of income.
After a certain "threshold" level of income, however, higher than that
of the urban and rural poor, there may be a sharp increase in household
consumption as access to new services provided by electricity is achieved
(see below page 18).

This lesser proportionate increase in gross energy inputs for
domestic purposes as incomes rise is associated with a changing pattern of
fuel use, from noncommercial to commercial fuels. In Pakistan, for
example, as incomes rise, the proportion of expenditure on fuelwood, dungcakes and kerosine falls very rapidly. Electricity, on the other hand,
accounts for a rapidly rising share in each income group. Similarly, in
the Indian cities, comsumption of noncommercial fuels falls with rising
incomes; consumption of soft coke rises though less rapidly than income,
while the rise in electricity consumption frequently exceeds the rise in
income. And in Mexico City as incomes rise, wood and coal are no longer
used, kerosine declines rapidly and electricity and gas provide roughly
one-half each of total consumption.

On the basis of these surveys, rising incomes appear to lead to
substitution of commercial for noncommercial fuels. To some extent this
is a question of availability; in urban areas "noncommercial" fuels are
either not available or must be purchased, thus pushing consumers in the
direction of the more efficient commercial fuels. Commercial fuels are
also often more convenient to handle and use. From the data presented
here it appears that the first step is an increased consumption of kerosine, but this in turn is abandoned in favor of electricity and, where
available, gas (usually bottled gas).

Household Budget Surveys

The relationship between energy consumption and income at different income levels can also be analyzed from household budget surveys. In this case energy consumption is measured in value terms, which takes into account the use of more efficient and more expensive forms of energy such as kerosine and electricity.

These surveys indicate fairly consistently that in both urban and rural areas, expenditure on fuel and light increases as income rises, though less rapidly than the rise in income. In other words the percentage of income spent on fuel and light declines as incomes rise. Typically in the upper income brackets, expenditure on fuel and light accounts for about 2-3 percent of expenditures, but in the lower income ranges the proportion is subtantially higher. In rural areas of some states of India, for example, expenditures on fuel and light may account for as much as 19 percent of total consumer expenditure though 10 percent is more typical (India: National Sample Survey, 1975). At these levels, expenditure on fuel and light is second in size after expenditures on food and is virtually the only other expenditure apart from food.

The Overseas Development Council's case study of "Energy Needs and Tasks Among the Urban Poor in Ouagadougou" indicated that purchases of fuelwood represented 30 percent of family expenditures. As the demand for fuelwood is believed in many areas to be highly seasonal--that is, it is used only when other forms of fuel, chiefly crop wastes, are not available--this exceptionally high proportion may not be typical of annual expenditures. In Colombia it is estimated that 10-20 percent of annual income is spent on fuels for domestic consumption. In other Latin American countries the proportion is somewhat less--5 to 8 percent.

The changing pattern of fuel consumption as incomes rise is confirmed by those household surveys which give expenditure by fuel, including imputed expenditure for noncommercial fuels. In Pakistan, for example, firewood and dungcakes account for 80 percent of total exenditure on energy items by the poorest groups. Kerosine accounts for about 10 percent and, to put the small quantities purchased into perspective, matches for 5 percent. The pattern of energy consumption begins to change only at higher income groups. Firewood, dungcakes, and kerosine all decline in relative importance and electricity shoots up to account for 35 percent of the total. Equally, among the rural poor of Sudan (see household budget survey of Sudan, Gezira-Manafil) energy demands shift to commercial fuels, charcoal, and particularly kerosine with rising income. But electricity consumption is restricted to the middle and higher rural income groups.

Role of Electricity

The advent of electricity is clearly of importance, if not at present then in the future, when rising incomes will enable a larger proportion of the poor to have access to electricity supplies. This raises the question: What is the effect of the introduction of electricity on total energy consumption? Does it substitute for less efficient forms of fuel and thus perform the same range of energy services as before with less gross energy input and posssibly with less deleterious environmental effect if wood is the fuel replaced, or does it, by extending the range of services demanded, increase gross energy inputs?

The Pakistan study concludes that "electrification seems to reduce the relative popularity of major alternative energy sources. A caveat for kerosine is that whereas electrification increased the popularity of kerosine for cooking, this effect is more than offset by electrification's sharply reducing the popularity of kerosine for lighting." Again, from the same report, "Electrified households use significantly less of each major fuel and of all fuels combined than nonelectrified households."

So far as it goes, therefore, this study suggests that electrification leads to a reduction in energy inputs by the household, the savings at the final consumption level obtained from switching from traditional fuels being greater than the extra electricity consumption occurring through its use in new energy services. This may be a reasonable conclusion at low levels of income where lack of resources precludes the purchase of electrical appliances. As incomes rise, however, the new uses may swamp the substitution effect.

Appliance Ownership

Data on appliance ownership is very sketchy for these countries as indeed it is for developed countries. The Calcutta Survey indicates that among the poorest of the urban poor, appliances are limited to a chula (stove), occasionally a kerosine stove, and some kerosine and electric lamps. As incomes rise the chula remains the major form of cooking stove, but is supplemented by kerosine stoves and then at higher income levels by gas and electric stoves. Again, as income rises, electric lighting is substituted for kerosine lamps. With regard to other appliances, first radios, fans and irons are acquired, and then refrigerators and air conditioners.

The family budget survey of Brazil bears out the same pattern, although even at the lowest income levels appliance ownership is much more widespread than in India. For example, in Porto Alegre, of the poorest 20 percent,

more than half possessed radios. There was also some ownership of appliances
such as sewing machines, irons and fans in this group.

Recent observations from a variety of sources suggest that in
both rural and urban areas, radios powered by batteries--which are not
included in energy consumption data--are widely used. In urban areas
of Latin America, where electricity is more widespread, television sets
are owned even by those with modest incomes. Such TV sets are
frequently used to yield income by charging neighbors for viewing.

Energy Efficiencies

The third component of the energy consumption system is the efficiency
with which these fuels are used. Traditional methods of cooking are carried
out at efficiencies estimated at 10 percent or less though the overall efficiency of a system as rudimentary as an open fire may be higher than the low
levels assumed if only cooking is considered. Dying embers are used for a
succession of energy using tasks requiring less high quality heat--heating
of water for washing, ironing, and so forth--in very much the same process
of matching quality of energy supply to energy using tasks which is urged in
developed countries.

Even allowing for some underestimation of system inefficiencies, these
low efficiences are at first sight surprising given the financial and other
costs of using energy. This question (which is taken up again in Chapter
IV) merits careful investigation as it implies that there are strong forces
at work inhibiting change.

For example, the costs of change may be exorbitant. As cooking fuel
changes from wood to charcoal, kerosine and gas or electricity, types of

stoves also change, becoming more expensive especially in initial outlay. Furthermore, different types of stoves require different cooking utensils which again add to the cost of adopting a new system. Existing uses may be more complex then is readily apparent. The open fire, whatever its seeming inefficiency, may in fact be highly appropriate for the desired end use. Little attention has been paid to these topics which may be of major importance in defining energy strategies, particularly in those areas highly dependent on wood fuel for cooking.

Another factor is that the cost of collecting fuelwood and dung appears to be borne largely by those groups--women and children--whose alternative occupations are particularly limited.

And finally, conservative attitudes no doubt play some part. Frequent mention is made in the literature of conservative views held in villages of the developing world which preclude the rapid introduction of new techniques. There is some evidence that those on the borderline of subsistence are, prudently enough, risk averse. On the other hand, views have been known to change quickly once circumstances indicate unambiguous need for change. (See Chapter IV).

The prospect of an increase in energy consumption as economic development proceeds focusses attention on the efficiency of fuel use. As we have seen from looking at the domestic sector, an increase in energy efficiency has taken place as consumers moved from noncommercial to commercial fuels. Though the effect was to increase the overall efficiency of the fuel supply system, the substitution of commercial for noncommercial (frequently petroleum based) fuels led to increased import bills. For the future there is every interest in exploring means of increasing efficiencies in all fuels, not only to minimize imports, but also, in the case of noncommercial fuels, to diminish the environmental costs of overuse. These costs, though domestically incurred, also have an indirect effect on the balance of payments. Thus, the diversion of dung or crop wastes from agriculture may require the import of chemical fertilizers or even food grains; and the destruction of ground cover through deforestation may also lead indirectly to the import of extra food supplies.

Energy Prices and Energy Consumption

So far in this chapter we have concentrated on the effect of different levels of income on energy consumption for domestic uses. Energy prices are also assumed to explain part of the differences in levels of energy consumption, in interfuel substitution, and in recent trends in energy consumption following the 1973/74 oil price rise. Insofar as energy prices can be shown to affect levels of consumption, then energy pricing provides a policy instrument for securing changes in energy consumption patterns.

Unfortunately, data on energy prices, where they exist, are very fragmentary, deal mainly with commercial fuels, and in any event are difficult to compare. Furthermore there is a conceptual difficulty in assigning a "price" to those non-commercial fuels which are not traded.

Further research would probably yield data on electricity prices in different regions. Indeed a World Bank Rural Electrification Sector Paper indicates that prices paid by rural dwellers despite subsidies, are substantially higher than those paid by urban dwellers. Data on energy in Latin America (CEPAL, 1975) indicates considerable variation in prices of all fuels among countries.

At any one time prices of kerosine, which benefit from a relatively organized distribution network, probably vary little from region to region within a country but may vary between large and small residential customers. Over time, however, they have changed sharply, with considerable variation from country to country. Table II-4 gives data on retail prices of kerosine from 1972 to 1976. As they have been converted to U.S. cents at current exchange rates they do not give an entirely accurate picture of costs in local currencies. But the data are adequate to point out the differences in experience between countries. In several countries, kerosine prices changed very little despite the fourfold rise in crude oil prices. In others, kerosine prices (and also bottled gas prices) frequently doubled. As inflation rates were high in these years the real rise in kerosine prices might differ considerably from the figures shown.[17]

This experience points to a widespread feature of energy pricing in developing countries--price control and subsidy of fuels used particularly by the domestic consumer. The subsidies in rural electrification are particularly high. The World Bank Rural Electrification paper for example gives a discrepancy of 2-6 cents per kilowatt hour between average costs and average prices (based on a study of rural electrification in El Salvador). Kerosine is also heavily subsidized in many countries, as table II-4 suggests.

---

[17]See also "An Examination of Changes in the Retail Price and Taxation of Petroleum Products in Developing Countries (July 1973-July 1974)", Katrine Saito, Development Economics Department, IBRD.

Table II-4.   Prices of Kerosine in Selected Countries, 1972 and 1976.
(U.S. cents per U.S. gallon)

	July 1972	July 1976
Bolivia	8.0	5.6
Brazil	31.7	75.0
Colombia	12.5	19.8
El Salvador	18.0	48.0
Ghana	22.8	87.0
India	30.6	54.6
Indonesia	7.5	16.4
Iran	12.4	13.4
Jamaica	16.4	32.5
Kenya	33.3	64.0
Mexico	10.3	6.0
Pakistan	15.8	33.3
Philippines	14.0	54.0
Sri Lanka	14.2	46.7 (July 1975)
Thailand	34.0	54.0

Source: International Petroleum Annual 1972 and 1976 editions
(table 10), U.S. Department of the Interior.

Adequacy of Consumption Levels

On the basis of the foregoing analysis, is the existing consumption
of the rural and urban poor "adequate?" The question is: adequate for
what? A number of studies[18] have put an approximate figure of--9-12 GJ
(0.3-0.4 tce) per annum (including "productive" uses) as the amount of
energy needed for the minimum provision of food and shelter, but this probably underestimates needs for those areas which require some space heating.
Under this criterion, it seems that in most of the areas we have considered,
energy consumption is barely adequate for minimum subsistence at the present
time using existing energy systems. Admittedly, data are of such poor
quality that this conclusion must be considered relative, but two further
considerations must be borne in mind. The first is that in some of the
rural areas already close to subsistence level, supplies (particularly to
the poor) may be dwindling due to deforestation or to changing availability
of animal and vegetable wastes due to new agricultural practices. The
second is that increasing population density will put pressure on fuelwood
and other biomass supplies. Once population exceeds a critical density,
shortages could conceivably develop very rapidly. The maintenance of even
barely adequate energy subsistence levels could therefore in some cases be
tenuous. Furthermore, minimal though this consumption is, it represents a
significant part of total expenditures in urban areas and often a significant part of the working day in rural areas. In both cases the provision of
even subsistence levels of energy consumption is a drain on the resources,
financial or otherwise, of the urban and rural poor.

---

[18]A. Makhijani and A. Poole, Energy and Agriculture in the Third
World, (Ballinger Publishing Co., Cambridge, Mass., 1975); J. Parikh, Energy
and Development (World Bank, PUN 43, Washington, D.C. 1977).

In the future, it can be anticipated that energy requirements will increase. Recent emphasis in development strategies has been placed on the provision of basic needs, variously defined, but usually including adequate food, shelter, and water.[19] Energy is rarely included in this list though its presence is implicit in the other needs. Thus an increased amount of food might require more cooking fuels, and services such as the provision of improved water and housing embody significant amounts of energy. So far, however, there appears to have been little effort to quantify this implicit energy content. The Brookhaven report is an exception.[20] It estimates that the consumption levels for most of the developing world including productive uses need to triple in order to secure an adequate life with some opportunity for improved health and well-being. This order of magnitude agrees with the results of Reddy and Prasad who estimate 43 GJ to be the "minimum requirement for a satisfactory life."[21]

Summary

The purpose of this chapter has been to derive a picture of domestic energy consumption of the urban and rural poor as they are at present, and as they might be expected to develop.

---

[19]Paul Streeten and Shahid Burke, "Basic Needs; Some Issues," World Development vol. 6, no. 3 (1978), pp. 411-421.

[20]Palmedo, Philip F., Robert Nathans, Edward Beardsworth, and Samuel Hale, Jr., Energy Needs, Uses and Resources in Developing Countries, report to USAID (Upton, N.Y., Brookhaven National Laboratory, March 1978).

[21]Amulya K. Reddy and K. Krishna Prasad "Technological Alternatives and the Indian Energy Crises," National Seminar on Energy, March 1976, Administrative Staff College of India, Hyderabad.

From the rudimentary data available, it appears that energy consumption by the rural and urban poor in much of Africa and Asia amounts to about 10 GJ (0.3 tons coal equivalent) per capita annually, an amount using existing energy systems considered to be barely adequate for subsistence at this time. In Latin America, it appears to be substantially higher. On the basis of the studies quoted here these seems to be little difference in consumption levels between the rural and urban poor. In Africa and Asia, a substantial proportion of total consumption is noncommercial fuels. This proportion is much higher in rural areas and, given the low rural energy efficiencies, particularly in cooking, of using noncommercial fuels, may account for the lack of difference between rural and urban consumption despite the generally higher urban incomes.

A further tentative conclusion is that for similar reasons, related to the changing efficiency of the fuel supply system, energy consumption measured in quantity terms rises by less than the rise in income at lower income levels at least. As incomes rise, there is a tendency to switch to more efficient fuels in a manner analogous to the contrast in energy consumption patterns between urban and rural areas. Thus a rising demand for energy services is accommodated by a less than proportionate gross energy input. The rise in energy consumption measured by expenditure is however much sharper than the increase in gross energy input since the increased efficiency of fuels tends to be reflected in higher prices. Even here, however, the increase in expenditures on energy items appears from a variety of sources to be substantially less than the rise in income.

Chapter III

COST FACTORS IN RENEWABLE SOURCES

Various conventional and unconventional alternatives can in principle be exploited to supply the energy needs of the poor in developing countries. But oil costs and foreign exchange problems, together with growing problems associated with sustaining supplies of traditional fuels suggest a strong emphasis on newer types of supply sources and new approaches to older ones. The analytic problem of assessing feasibilities is exacerbated by the need to consider future, presumably higher fossil energy prices that are not reflected in current costs to the consumer--and may indeed be marked by the common national practice of subsidizing such household fuel as kerosine.

For each developing area, the choice of energy supply systems depends on local climate, resources, economy, and other variables. Determining the suitability of a particular type of energy supply is especially difficult for the newer, nonconventional renewable resources; but for many developing areas, even standard questions, such as the costs of rural electrification, have not yet been answered. For many developing areas, the all-important question of the price of competing fuels such as kerosine or central station electricity cannot yet be specified in many cases. Furthermore, institutional constraints and complex economic interactions can be as important as simple economic feasibility; these problems are analyzed more thoroughly in Chapters IV and V. Nonetheless, this chapter tries to point out some relevant quantitative and qualitative features of costs and resources.

Biogas

Biogas is generated by allowing organic matter of various kinds to decay in oxygen-poor environments; it is identical to the marsh gas of freshwater wetlands. Any organic waste containing carbon, hydrogen, and oxygen may be a suitable candidate for biogas production.[1]

Under the action of naturally occurring bacterial flora of various kinds, the very long organic chains containing carbon, hydrogen, and oxygen, together with some other compounds--in particular nitrogen--are dissociated first into their constitutent sugars and then transformed by another set of bacteria into various alcohols and acids. Finally, some of these alcohols and acids are transformed into methane, carbon dioxide and other trace gases (NAS, 1977, p. 27) with the energetically useful part-- methane--typically making up 60 to 70 percent of the total. Therefore, the resulting gas has a fairly high heat content per volume, 600-700 Btu per cubic foot or 22-26 gigajoules per cubic meter (Loehr, in Brown, 1978, p. 131, 140).

The product gas is then an energetically close substitute for natural gas and can be piped economically for distances of interest for decentralized community use. Major maintenance can be minimal, with only yearly painting of a metal gasholder as a necessary task, and an unobjectionable residue is produced which can be used for fertilizer. Since the basic products are compounds of carbon and hydrogen, most of the nitrogen--the fertilizing agent--is retained, perhaps 80 percent (NAS, 1977, p. 50). As with natural gas, there is the possiblility of safety problems, since methane is explosive when mixed with air in proportions of 5-15 percent by volume (NAS, 1977, p. 99).

---

[1]However, a certain nitrogen content is required, and manures or other materials containing nitrogen may have to be added to sawdust and some types of crop residues that are nitrogen-deficient (Loehr, in Brown, 1978, p.133).

Some cost estimates are available but since costs are somewhat uncertain for future use, especially on a wider scale, it is of interest also to compare energy balances. That is, organic waste could be utilized directly for fuel in a fire, rather than converted into biogas. Indeed, there is some net energy loss in the conversion. If it is assumed that one metric ton of dry manure possesses 16.7 gigajoules of energy, and that the biogas produced by the anaerobic decomposition of this manure would capture 55 percent or about 9.2 gigajoules, then if this gas is burned in a stove with an efficiency of 48 percent, the net energy delivered to the end use would be about 4.4 gigajoules (Goldemberg in Appendix IV, section C, ODC, 1978). However, the 16.7 gigajoules in the original dung would be unlikely to be delivered efficiently to an end use by burning. Efficiencies in primitive stoves and open fires have been estimated at 10 percent, which would mean that in practice only about 1.7 gigajoules in the original dung might be delivered to the end use. While gas yields vary in practice, biogas conversion could therefore double or at least match the delivered end-use energy available from the animal wastes.

Much of the activity in the development of biogas has been in India. Some figures for 10 projects in Uttar Pradesh show costs ranging from 2.6-6.7 rupees per thousand feet of gas produced, or $0.77-2.0 (1975 dollars) per gigajoule [2](NAS, 1977, table 1-7). This calculation appears to be consistent with other Indian model calculations (NAS, 1977, Appendix II). The latter show that gas sold at a price of $2.80 per gigajoules provides the enterprise with a substantial profit. On the basis that the costs of

---

[2]Assuming an exchange ratio of 8 rupes to one U.S. dollar, and 0.680 gigajoules per thousand cubic feet, and taking the ratio of 1967 dollars to 1975 dollars as 1/1.6.

the systems are about equal to the gas revenues, and another equal contribution to revenues comes from the sale of residues as manure, the real costs
(with no profit) appear to fall within the range of the other estimates, at
about $1.40/GJ.

Another Indian estimate gives the (1973) cost of a 10 cubic meter
volume gas plant as Rs. 2075, with annual capital charges of Rs. 395
(Kashkari, 1975, pp. 86 ff). If the dung required per plant-year were
used instead for fuel, its value would be 338 rupees. Against this is
income from gas sales of 378 rupees (at 10 rupees per 29 cubic meters) and
480 rupees from manure based on additional wastes enriched with the gas
plant residue. At 24 gigajoules per thousand cubic meters, the price of
the gas from this plant is about 14 rupees per gigajoule, or at 8 rupees
to the dollar, approximately $1.80 per gigajoule. Again, the gas could be
sold more cheaply at a cost, with no profit, of $1.20/GJ. Another estimate
of costs for Indian biogas plants ranges from $1.80/GJ for a 5000 ft^3
plant to $3.20/GJ for a 60 ft^3 plant (Prasad, 1974).

Experience in Pakistan, for a ten cubic meter biogas plant of the
Chinese type, requiring five head of cattle, and a capital cost (at 10
rupees = $1.00) of approximately $290, leads to estimates of yearly costs
of approximately $50.00 based on a thirty year life of the plant, revenues
from gas of $40.00, and fertilizer of $21.00, giving a net profit of some
$10.00 (Pakistan, 1977, pp. 17-18). The price of gas from this plant is
approximately $0.95 per gigajoule; if sold at cost with no profit, it
could be sold at close to $0.70/GJ.

Model estimates made for Tanzania have figured that cooking and
lighting could be supplied by direct gas use in villages at about 12 mills

per kilowatt hour or $3.3 per gigajoule[3] (Tanzania, 1978, p. 32); this

cost, however, does not include the cost of gathering dung for the

feedstock. If lighting were provided by electricity from gas, however, the

estimated costs are much larger, 220 mills per kilowatt hour or $61 per

gigajoule. Other estimates have put the cost of electricity from biogas at

51 mills per kilowatt hour or more (ODC, 1978, Appendix IV, quoting Tyner

and Adams). These estimates are somewhat higher than those made for a pro-

ject in Sri Lanka (Allison, 1978). There the middle-range estimate cost

from a combination wind, solar, and biogas system was put at 121 mills per

kilowatt hour (see below, p. 59); however, the biogas element was said to be

the cheapest of the three, perhaps producing power at half the cost of the

other methods (Allison, private communication).

Other trials of biogas usage that are of interest are those in China.

There are said to be more than 4 million biogas units in China used for

cooking and lighting (Smil, 1977). The gas from a typical unit is distri-

buted under pressure at a distance of 10 to 20 meters to stoves and lamps.

Reinforced concrete is used for larger tanks, but for small biogas tanks,

local materials are often used. For a typical 10 cubic meter tank, a cost

of 3040 yuan ($15-$20?) has been estimated. Smaller tanks are costed at

approximately 10 yuan.

The costs quoted above for biogas plants--$0.7 to $3/GJ--although often

higher-priced than firewood or waste (see below), appear to be competitive

with other sources, such as kerosine--at perhaps $3 to $6 per gigajoule

delivered to typical developing country villages (neglecting subsidies:

compare table II-4 above). Also, the amount of the resource in animal

---

[3] 10 mills/kWh - $0.10/kWh = $2.78/GJ.

wastes potentially available for biogas usage can be rather large. It has
been estimated (Kashkari, 1975, p. 86 ff) that the amount available in
India in the year 1975-1976 was 324 million dry tons (p. 94). The order of
magnitude of energy potentially available is then about 5.5 billion gigajoules.

Data on this supply option appear relatively adequate from a narrowly
technical point of view. A considerable amount of research and a large
number of pilot projects, especially in India, have been carried out for use
of biogas for cooking and lighting, and results of the allegedly successful
experience in China with low capital cost designs using fixed concrete
gasholders, instead of the metal floating gasholder, are now being transferred to other countries such as Pakistan. But some reports have been made
of plants not used or underutilized because of cold weather failures or lack
of wastes, and data on general user acceptance is less than adequate.
Furthermore, data on the socioeconomic problems of usage are also less
available. For example, the equity of dung collection enters: if dung were
a free good and became commercial subsequently, the supply of fuel to the
rural poor could decrease on a practical basis. Plant ownership equity
problems can also arise, since the minimum size of a practical tank may be
too large for the amounts of dung or other residues that are available to
the average poor family. Furthermore, distribution of gas in rural areas
and the availability of biomass supplies in urban areas remain as problems
to be investigated. (See Chapter IV for a fuller discussion of these
problems.)

Solar

Since cooking needs loom so large in the energy requirements for households in developing countries, the possibility of cooking with the direct use

of active solar energy is intriguing. Problems of a combined technical and sociological nature arise, however. Flat plate collectors are the easiest and cheapest to use but only relatively low temperatures (140°C) are usually obtained with them (Walton, 1978, p. 28 ff). Concentrating collectors are more expensive and somewhat more awkward to use, in that the sun's rays must be focussed on the cooking utensil. Even more serious, solar cooking without some storage or transfer mechanisms must be done outside and in the daytime. It is possible to transfer solar heat inside with steam systems or to store the solar energy in oil or eutectic salts, or possibly in more exotic ways such as utilizing the heat of dissolution of acid in water. However, all these solutions add to the costs and quite possibly to the inconvenience of solar cooking.

In spite of these problems, solar cooking might be a useful last resort in regions where fuel is very expensive. Early trials in India, Morocco, and Mexico failed to gain user acceptance, although one reviewer was unable to find documentation of these reported failures. Some have considered trials by a University of Wisconsin team in Mexico in 1958 and 1961 (see Chapter IV below), though failures in practice, as successful in principle, given the relatively low prices of alternative fuels at that time (Walton, 1978, pp. 58-61). However, the pilot project did point out the necessity for an in-depth and on-the-spot educational program to introduce the cookers to the locality. A Danish organization ("Danchurchaid") has introduced 250 solar cookers in Upper Volta in a similar program. Reportedly, 2,300 solar stoves are being used in Honan province, China (Gopalakrishnan, 1978). In addition, many research institutions, such as that in Bamako, Mali, will be engaged in trial introductions of solar cookers. Chapter IV below discusses user acceptance problems in such projects at more length.

Costs of solar cookers vary greatly, as reportedly do efficiencies. A recent survey (Walton, 1978, p. 53, Table V) showed various models in the $7 to $18 range; however, all of these were marked "poor" for baking. Others, such as the Prata model at $35 was marked "good" for baking, but "fair" for stewing and frying. Costs could be lowered by constructing a fixed cooker with cheap materials; however, these cookers are somewhat inflexible in operation. Fairly inexpensive parabolic reflectors were made from plastic in the Mexican experiment utilizing 8-22 hours of local labor and $15 worth of materials (Walton, 1978, pp. 55-58). Old data on India report prices for cookers of $15 (Stead, 1957), while the Ghai cooker introduced there was costed at $14-18 (Walton, 1978, p. 53). Limited data on use in China indicate that a folding type of solar stove, used in Kansu province, costs 15 yuan (about $7.50?) (Smil, 1977a).

Further functions related to rural life in villages can be effected with direct use of the sun. Solar collectors are particularly well suited to crop drying because of the low temperatures required. Solar heat can also be of use in providing a clean water supply, either by distilling water in basins covered by, for example, sloping sheets of glass (Lof in Brown, 1978, pp. 36-37), or by providing pumping for potable water supplies or for irrigation. Flat plate pumps exist, but tend to be rather expensive: for example, $25,000 per kilowatt of mechanical power provided (Walton, 1978, p. 11). Concentrating collectors, such as parabolic dish collectors delivering temperatures of over 300° C to a heat engine, can potentially produce mechanical energy more economically. It is projected that one kind of such collector on a production basis could produce mechanical power at a capital cost of $5,000 per kilowatt (Walton, 1978, p. 20).

Space heating and water heating can of course be accomplished by active solar means, while passive solar schemes such as clever housing design are of course already familiar in many developing areas. In Australia, in particular, a well established technology for small (180 liter) water systems exists (NAS, 1972, p. 16, and Brown, 1978, pp. 27-42). Solar refrigeration has been proposed for the refrigeration of fish in theoretical calculations for Tanzania (Tanzania, 1978, p. 46), at estimated costs of approximately 12 cents per kilowatt hour.

Another possibility for household energy from solar is photovoltaic electric power. One of the big advantages of photovoltaic power is its engineering simplicity. Units are or should be designed to be modular, so that power can still be produced if elements are damaged. Replacing damaged elements and regular replacement of auxiliary batteries every three to five years, are, however, continuing costs that must be considered (NAS, 1976, p. 103). The cost of energy from photovoltaic cells is presently rather large. But, even at present prices photovoltaic cells are an option for small amounts of electricity for educational TV receivers, operation of audio-visual equipment, and refrigerators in small rural health centers. It has been estimated that at a cost of $20 per peak watt--which can be easily achieved at present--power from photovoltaic cells for typical installations might be $5.50 per kilowatt hour (Weiss, 1976, p. 5). While expensive, these costs are cheaper than typical costs in the Ivory Coast of power from batteries of about $12 per kilowatt hour (Weiss, 1976, p. 4). For comparison, gasoline generators are now being used in one application in Malaysia to operate educational TV receivers: energy costs are $4 per

kilowatt hour for gasoline delivered at present prices of 50 cents per
gallon, but would be significantly more if future gasoline prices were
higher.

Photovoltaics have smaller costs per kilowatt when larger amounts of
electricity are supplied than when used only for educational TV; however,
costs are still relatively large in general compared to other sources. In
theoretical studies for Tanzania (Tanzania, 1978, p. 37), PV arrays supplying
300 kilowatt hours daily would deliver electricity at about $1.20 per kilo-
watt hour at a $20 per peak watt array cost. If, as hoped, prices of photo-
electric arrays eventually fall to about 50 cents per peak watt, then the
calculation shows the electricity could be sold for about 10 cents per
kilowatt hour, which is in the competitive range under present local conditions. If indeed array costs do come down, an entirely different set of
uses for photovoltaic--for example, for lighting or for small 1/4 horse-power
DC water pumps (NAS, 1976, p. 96)--could achieve feasibility.

Other calculations have been carried out for a hypothetical village in
India. Costs of photovoltaic, compared to other sources, as usual depend on
the size and pattern of the load. For a motorized potable water supply, the
photovoltaic costs at 50 cents per peak watt could be $455, or 12 cents per
kWh. This compares with gasoline generation costs, at current prices, of
$335 per year or 9 cents per kWh. If an increment were added to supply a
rice huller, powered by either photovoltaic or by diesel, the systems cost
would be the same, or about $1,075 per year additional; taking load factors
into account, unit costs for this increment would be 12 cents per kWh. If in
addition, some lighting and educational TV were added, a photovoltaic array

could supply the load at a total cost of $1,540 per year and a unit cost of 14 cents per kWh, compared to costs for a combination of gasoline and diesel engines and generators of $1,277 per year (Smith, 1977, pp. 50 ff).

Therefore, future costs for small loads in isolated places may not be exorbitant for PV arrays; and for some restricted purposes, such as communications, photovoltaics may be practical at present. However, certain institutional requirements stand out (Weiss, 1976). Maintenance must be really almost unnecessary in order to convince users of this claimed qualitative advantage of the system. In addition, in order to avoid consumer uncertainties, usual warranty periods might need to be extended. Finally, the initial capital costs of the photovoltaics are very high. For the Ivory Coast, present-day photovoltaics to operate one educational TV set would probably cost $2,000 much greater than the cost of primary cells (batteries) at $750, even though the operating costs upon an annualized basis could well be less (see above) for the photovoltaics. Therefore availability of credit is an important requirement for market penetration.

Solar thermal generators, using the sun's heat to generate steam or some other vapor in order to drive ordinary turbine generators, could also be used to supply electricity. In fact, one demonstration project in Sri Lanka sponsored by UNEP combines both a solar thermal and photovoltaic systems and a wind generator with a backup biogas generator to generate electricity for lighting and other purposes in a small village (Allison, 1978). The unit cost of energy from the projected system is, according to a lower estimate of capital costs of $2,000 per kilowatt, 48.6 mills per kilowatt hour. At the more probable eventual capital cost of $5,000 per kilowatt, the energy cost would be 121 mills per kilowatt hour. Even this compares favorably with

costs for diesel generation of 113 mills per kilowatt hour at present prices
of 60 cents per gallon for diesel fuel, and 156 mills per kilowatt hour at
$1.20 per gallon (H.J. Allison, private communication).

Small-Scale Hydroelectric

Small-scale hydroelectric facilities can supply in principle significant
amounts of electricity for irrigation or potable water pumping, lighting, or
health or educational purposes. The total potential amount of such a
resource is very poorly documented but is apt to be large. For Brazil, the
total amount of potential capacity has been estimated at 330 gigawatts (ODC,
1978, Appendix IV, section D). The total is large because rather small heads
of water can be utilized: a 100-kilowatt facility, estimated in the local
context to be enough to supply about 100 households, could be installed in a
waterfall with only 6 meters head and a 1.5 cubic meter per second flow (ODC,
1978, Appendix IV, section D).

In the context of developing areas, relevant development of this supply
source has occurred in China (Smil, 1977a). Three hundred thirty megawatts
were reported on line in 1959 from this source, with a weighted average of 42
kilowatts per installation; after a hiatus, interest has been renewed during
the last decade, but not many data appear to be available. Load factors are
reported low, with lighting loads typically characterized by one or two 15-
or 40-watt bulbs per house; however, power is also used for local industries,
irrigation, threshing and milling, fodder crushing, oil extraction, and
timber sawing. As with any hydroelectric installations, the ensuing regula-
tion of water supply may be an important related benefit.

Costs of mini-hydro installations vary widely. One fragmentary cost figure for China of a 0.6 kilowatt unit costing 300 yuan (about $150) has been cited (Ermenc in Brown, 1978, p. 99). Other costs have been given as about $500 per kilowatt for 25 kilowatts or greater, with costs rising to $1,000 per kilowatt at capacities between 10 and 15 kilowatts and to over $3,000 per kilowatt at capacities of 5 kilowatts; but these estimates do not include the cost of installation or of dams. Theoretical estimates for Tanzania took $500 per kilowatt as the cost of generators and turbines, but also considered extra costs from power conditioning at $750 per kilowatt and batteries at $800 per kilowatt hour; net costs of electricity for various options came out between 31 and 97 mills per kilowatt hour (Tanzania, 1978, p. 30). Again, costs of dams and penstocks were not included. The economic analysis of a "micro-hydel" unit in Pakistan give a capital cost of about $1,600, with yearly cost of approximately $400, and a unit cost of about 45 mills per kilowatt hour (Pakistan, 1977, pp. 16-17). A plan for a rural factory operation in Nepal has been costed at about 100 mills per kWh (Asia, 1977, p. 5). Costs in the United States for systems have been estimated in the range of $700 to $1,200 in installed costs per kilowatt (NESP, 1979, Chap. 10); Department of Energy statements have estimated 20 to 25 mills per kilowatt hour as an average unit cost of electricity from a small-scale hydro plant for U.S. load factors and streamflows.

Mini-hydro costs will probably decrease as the technology matures but will of course remain variable. But U.S. experience and even the present developing country present costs quoted above of 30-100 mills per kWh suggest that this source can be competitive in areas of high central power station electricity costs. However, region-dependent problems, such as seasonal flow, must be considered (ODC, 1977, p. 19).

Institutional aspects, such as the distribution of power and the availability of maintenance skills at a local level, may be of special importance for this option.

Most developing area estimates also do not take into account the environmental effects, which are the major concern in the United States. Indeed, most estimates of mini-hydro in the United States presuppose using existing dams where environmental effects are already well established. Admittedly, environmental goods may be valued less highly in developing areas, while water control for nonenergy purposes may on occasion be even more highly valued than energy uses. Nevertheless, environmental damage to aquatic species and other ecological effects must still be considered in any analysis.

Wind

Windmills for pumping water and supplying mechanical and therefore electrical energy of various sorts is an established technology. In addition, the possibility of using local materials is always present. A type of "Cretan sailmill" has been used to pump water for irrigation in a semi-arid region in Ethiopia (ODC, 1977, Appendix III, p. 93); the cost of such sailmills was reported as $375. Within the past decades, the National Aeronautical Lab at Bangalore, India produced 200 12-blade fan-type windmills for water pumping. An 8-meter diameter sail wing windmill has been tested in Madurai, India: it is constructed from a 1-meter diameter bullock cartwheel and three bamboo poles, nylon cord, and cloth sails (Kashkari, 1975, p. 192). Indigenous wind technology also exists in Thailand, where windmill driven "water ladders" have been utilized (NAS, 1976, p. 114).

Windmills can of course also generate electricity, but the electric option is relatively complicated and requires in general more engineering expertise for maintenance. Indeed, maintenance and distribution system management problems could form severe obstacles to the use of wind electric generators in developing areas. In addition, at least with present designs, there seems to exist a fairly large economy of scale in producting wind converters (NESP, 1979, Chap. 10). However, even small units of 15-18 kilowatts have been quoted at as little as $500 to $600 per kilowatt without, however, including the cost of the towers. Unit costs for small applications are difficult to obtain. However, for one theoretical study in Tanzania (Tanzania, 1978) the unit cost for wind-generated electricity on a small scale was put at 180 mills per kilowatt hour. It should be noted that costs of 62.5 mills per kWh have been reported for some small wind systems in the United States (NESP, 1979, Chap. 11); however, these costs are dependent on being hooked into existing utility grids and therefore relatively high load factors. Other U.S. theoretical estimates, including some storage, show costs ranging above and below 40 mills/kWh (Lovins, 1978, p. 502).

One of the biggest problems with wind is its irregularity both in time and space. Many developing areas, such as south Asia, are not characterized by high prevailing speed winds. However, if winds of 9-17 kilometers per hour are taken as average (Tewari in Brown, 1978, p. 85) then a 20-25 kilometer per hour rated windmill would be appropriate: such windmills could be of a reasonable diameter (for example, less than 12 meters) if they were to irrigate one hectare. Nevertheless, wind applications in LDCs might require more emphasis on low-wind speed technology.

Fuelwood and Wastes

The world's forest are a vast resource, not only for energy, but also
for ecological balance, prevention of erosion, and supply of timber. The
size of the tropical forests, for example, is very large, especially relative
to some regional needs. It has been calculated that 10 percent of the tropical forest in Africa could provide, with careful use, enough fuel to
sustain future needs on that continent, even admitting a considerable growth
in demand in firewood consumption for the next 20 years (French, 1978,
quoting Earl). Even the potential output of wood waste can be large; this
potential energy source has been identified in Ghana as being greater than
that consumed in the entire present national power production (French, 1978,
quoting Powell). Nevertheless, other regions will be expected to experience
problems, as world statistics show. The total amount of forest in developing
areas as of 1963 (Openshaw, 1977, p. 14, table 9) has been estimated at 2.04
billion hectares of which 1.05 billion are classified as "unproductive." At
81 cubic meters and 102 cubic meters--for coniferous and non-coniferous trees
respectively--of growing stock of wood per hectare, the total growing stock
is some 201 billion cubic meters, with an estimated yearly increment of 4.1
billion cubic meters. However, it has been calculated that world harvesting
of wood for all purposes might well exceed twice that increment in the year
2000 (Openshaw, 1977, p. 15).

Furthermore, on a global basis, there appears to be evidence that the
total original world forest area of about 4 billion hectares has decreased by
500 million hectares during the decade 1963-1973 (WB-F, 1978, pp. 25-26). As
a countervailing force, it is estimated that there is a small but growing
movement toward tree farming on plantations, now estimated to cover 11
million hectares of forest area. In local situations, of course, the loss of

firewood has been severe: such tendencies have been seen in Pakistan, where now 25 percent of all commercial wood is imported, and firewood costs in the neighborhood of $30 per ton, or perhaps $1.50 per gigajoule (Draper, 1970). According to the now famous anecdotal example of Eckholm (1975, pp. 6-7), it now takes an entire day in some sections of Nepal to get wood, where a generation ago only one to two hours were required, and where the price of a load of wood in Kathmandu has risen several hundred percent since 1973.

Potential supply possibilities for the future depend of course on local climate, demography, and competing land uses. The World Bank has identified certain forestry development categories to be applied to developing nations, depending on the present status and future potential of the forest and the economic environment and planned population pressures (WB-F, 1978, pp. 31-33). Obviously, the possible set of supply strategies for "wood-abundant poor areas with severe population pressures," like the Ivory Coast and Colombia, are different than those for "over populated wood-deficient areas" such as India and the Indonesian island of Java.

Strategies to increase firewood potential vary. Introduction of new fast-growing tree varieties, such as the eucalyptus successfully introduced some 70 or 80 years ago by the Emperor Menelik II into Ethopia, can be a useful tactic. (ODC, 1977, p. 61). Comprehensive reforestation projects are increasingly taking into account the combined needs of fuelwood and logging for materials and pulp, as well as attendant erosion control benefits (Diaper, 1976). Other strategies are establishing wood plantations: a worldwide dedication of 1.3 billion hectares to wood plantations could conceivably produce 13 billion cubic meters of wood per year; however, such a strategy would require an investment of some $6 billion a year (Openshaw,

1976, p. 17). A final strategy is that of establishing village woodlots: it has been estimated that 73 hectares could support the needs of a Nepalese village of 250 (Asia, 1977, p. 12). Such woodlots, however, might have to be very extensive where needed most, that is, in marginal lands like the Sahel, where one hectare might be needed to support the firewood needs of each inhabitant (Jean Gorse, private communication).

Costs of firewood of course range widely. Despite the eucalyptus campaign, the costs of wood in the village of Debarek, Ethopia (ODC, 1977, p. 81) were reported at what is apparently the equivalent of $4 per cubic meter or 40 cents per gigajoule. One recently observed price of firewood in the Dominican Republic showed a value of $0.80/GJ (William Ramsay, prices observed by author). Reports from a number of urban locations in different sections of India showed an average price of $1.40/GJ, with a range of $0.80 (Karnataka) to $1.80 (Rajasthan) (von Oppen, 1978). For plantations, assuming costs of $565-$725 per hectare for planting and maintenance through a plantation's first year, the cost of firewood from such projects is about $10 per ton or about 50 cents per gigajoule (French, 1978, p. 9, quoting Weber). However, worldwide most fuelwood is not sold, but is gathered by household members from surrounding or even distant forests on a formal or informal "public goods" basis. Estimating the opportunity costs of such fuel is difficult.

The greatest problems with firewood, however, are not those of costs, but of the institutional difficulties of the usual kinds involved in public goods. Unless forestry schemes are commercialized, uncontrolled harvesting by the public for fuel is apt to destroy their effectiveness. For this reason, commercialization, new institutions in firewood management, or even developing substitutes for firewood appear to be the most promising options for supply strategies.

Vegetable wastes are an important source of fuel in many areas. As for
the animal wastes mentioned above, however, collection of wastes is
generally carried out on an informal basis and price data are difficult to
either obtain or to infer. The significance of such a resources, potentially 200 million tonnes in India (Revelle, 1976), or several billion gigajoules, is enormous, if not well-documented.

Charcoal and Other Pyrolytics

Charcoal-making is a well-established technology that can be carried
out--although at low efficiencies--using primitive inexpensive kilns.
Depending on the methods used, perhaps 15 to 50 percent of the energy origi-
nally contained in the wood is retained in the charcoal. Balanced against
this energy loss is the greater compactness of charcoal, which reduces
transportation costs, and the fact that charcoal may be used some three and
a half to four times more efficiently in cooking than wood, depending again
on local circumstances (French, 1978, p. 11, quoting Earl and Uhart).

Charcoal use may, of course, be economically more feasible for use by
tbe urban poor; collection of fuelwood is likely to be more difficult in
suburban shanty towns than in rural areas. Pollution problems can of course
occur with either wood or charcoal, depending to a great extent on methods of
combustion; the precise environmental consequences of wood-charcoal mixes
need investigation.

Costs of charcoal are variable: for example, the 10 cents per kilogram
price quoted for a village in Ethopia (ODC, 1977, p. 61) corresponds probably
to over $3 per gigajoule. The question of efficiency of conversion may be
important from the point of view of energy balance. Unfortunately, efficient
kilns may present problems of capital allocation for some developing environ-

Table III-1. Quoted Cost Estimates for Some Energy Technologies, Fuels, and
Appliances

Technology, Fuel, or Appliance	Quoted Cost Estimates
Electric	
Photovoltaic cells (@ $20/peak watt)	$1-6 per kwh
Mini-hydro (excluding dam and penstock costs)	$0.03-0.10 per kwh
Wind generators	$0.04-0.18 per kwh
Diesel electricity	$0.10-.30 per kwh
Central station electricity (transmission and distribution cost only)	$0.007-0.13 per kwh
Other	
Biogas	$0.07-3 per GJ
Fuelwood	$0.40-2 per GJ
Kerosine	$3-6 per GJ
Solar cookers	$7-35 per unit

Source: See text.

ments; improved charcoal kilns of an economic scale have been quoted as costing in excess of $1,000 (French, 1978, p. 12, quoting Little and Uhart).

More advanced methods of wood distillation and pyrolysis recover not only charcoal but also pyrolytic oils that can also serve as fuel. Such systems would be relatively expensive; nevertheless, claims have been made for their economic feasibility (Tatom, 1976, p. 33). If suitable high-efficiency stoves for burning pyrolytic oils can be developed, the possibility arises for increasing by some 150 percent the amount of useful energy available from biomass (French, 1978, p. 12, quoting Tatom). In addition, the method would be applicable to a wide range of other agricultural and forest wastes; however, costs and feasibilities have yet to be determined.

Petroleum

The use of kerosine for cooking, lighting and other uses is presently an important constituent of energy supply for the poor in many developing countries. Liquid petroleum gas is also widely used. Diesel fuel and other petroleum products are also useful for other purposes related to household needs, such as the generation of electricity.

For oil importing countries, the price of kerosine and its availability are determined by the world price, by transportation costs, and by any possible foreign exchange difficulties the developing nation may be experiencing. Costs of distribution and transportation to be added to world petroleum product prices will vary a great deal. Subsidies can also produce widely varying prices (see table II-4 for kerosine figures). However, figures such as the 18 cents per liter for gasoline quoted for Bangladesh (Smith, 1977, p. 55) and the 60 cents a gallon for diesel fuel in Sri Lanka

(Allison, 1978) are consistent with surcharges of $2 or $3 per gigajoule for transportation, distribution, and refining costs over and above the world market price of crude oil, which presently is approximately $2.00 per gigajoule.

For the urban poor, especially, kerosine may still constitute an attractive supply alternative for household cooking and lighting, even taking into account oil crisis imperatives: long-term price trends are of course important here. Diesel generators are often the only source of electricity in remote areas. Recent workshop results for Tanzania (Tanzania, 1978, p. 47) assume a cost of approximately 280 mills per kilowatt hour for diesel unit of 500-kilowatt capacity; 113 mills was reported above for the Sri Lanka project. Such high costs are not unexpected for independent diesel units operating under fairly small load factors.

Central Station Electricity

Electricity is an exceedingly versatile source of power, both for industry and for household uses. However, electrification programs in developing areas have had somewhat mixed success. Despite the fact that, for example, 25 percent of the villages in India have been reported to "have electricity" (M&P, 1975, p. 22), the proportion of villagers using electricity tends to be low, the extent of use usually slowing greatly after 20 percent of the population becomes users. Nevertheless, due to the importance of electricity in the history of the development of the present industrialized countries, the feeling is often expressed that electricity is synonymous with a growing economy and society (Unti, 1972, p. 10). Electricity can serve to operate irrigation pumps and supply to an average village such as services as pure water and even power for radio, TV and other communications media (Unti, 1972, pp. 5 ff). However, even some advocates concede that while electricity may be very important to the central task of improving agricultural production, it has tended to be of secondary economic and social value in serving basic energy needs of the poor (Unti 1972, p. 12). For example, a survey in Bangladesh shows that less than 5 percent of the rural population in one electrified area used electricity for any purpose and that very little electricity was consumed for productive purposes other than powering tubewells (Smith, 1977a).

However, it should be noted that perhaps excessively great expectations have been had for the ability of programs of subsidized electric power to overcome distributional inequities. Other fuel supply sources—with the possible exception of highly subsidized fuelwood projects—will also not automatically overcome the problem of unequal economic development for different income classes.

Actual costs of electricity, while relatively large in some developing areas—due possibly partly to unfavorable economies of scale in generation—may hinge greatly on the high costs of transmission and distribution. For the entire electrical system, the problem of small load factors arises because expensive equipment must be kept idle during periods when little or no electrical demand exist. For example, in the course of the Tanzania workshop (Tanzania, 1978), the cost of transmitting and distributing electricity to a typical village presently 20 kilometers from an existing transmission line was estimated at 7 to 70 mills, depending on whether the load factor (fraction of capacity used) was 1 or 0.1. In addition, some 33 mills per kilowatt hour had to be added for the cost of transformers at the transmission line hookup point. Even for generating costs of say 20 mills per kilowatt hour, as is now typical in the United States (Schurr, 1979, chapter 8), extra transmission and distribution costs could make the delivery price of electrical energy quite high. For Bangladesh, one estimate (Smith, 1977, p. 55) has $25 per kilometer per kilowatt as the extra cost of adding transmission lines into a village. For a 20 kilometer hookup and a 10 percent capital charge rate, the extra cost of bringing 3 kW of electrical power from the point of the main transmission lines was 130 mills per kilowatt hour; since the load factors contemplated in this Bangladesh example are very small, this result is roughly consistent with the Tanzania result.

Various methods have been suggested for reducing these costs. It has been estimated that costs can be cut by a factor of 2 by using single-phase lines and wooden poles (Smith, 1977a). Another means is by adding higher voltage transmission lines: India now has 220 kilovolt lines and 400 kilovolt lines will be added next, and increases in voltage result in a relatively large decrease in the cost of transmission (Kashkari, 1975, p. 104). Another expedient has been suggested in Ethopia, where the use of capacitors instead of transformers to tap the grid is being investigated (Allison, private communication).

Transmission and distribution problems are of course much less important for supplying energy to the urban poor, where existing grids may provide a relatively inexpensive supply of energy.

Institutional aspects of introducing new electrical grids, should their use prove efficient for satisfying village end uses, still present problems. The pattern of REA-model loans through independent cooperatives and the reported success of electric cooperatives in India and in the Philippines (Unti, 1972, pp. 14, 16) suggest some methods of accomplishing these goals.

Conclusion

Many conceivable supply options exist for satisfying the household energy needs of the poor in developing countries. Table III-1 summarizes some of the rough estimates of costs reviewed above for various technologies, fuels, and appliances.

Even given the great uncertainty in the data now available, there remain great problems in feasibility assessment. The near- and mid-term prospects for the use of both the newer and the more conventional energy technologies depends very strongly on the actual and perceived costs and disadvantages of traditional fuels as greater usage and often decreasing availability of supply changes the explicit or implicit prices of these resources. Furthermore, many of the newer methods of satisfying supply requirements cannot be fully assessed for economic feasibility without further research and testing.

Of the new methods, biogas seems furthest along, and appears to be assured of some practical applications and perhaps a large role in supplying cooking fuel to rural inhabitants. Solar cookers suffer from lack of appropriateness to end uses that typically call for inside and nighttime cooking, and so sociological feasibility remains to be tested. Wind energy could provide potable water supplies for household use where conditions are suitable. Small hydroelectric facilities in some areas could provide power to rural areas at costs below that of electricity supplied by a national grid with low load factors and high transmission costs. Similarly, photovoltaic cells, even under present cost conditions, could supply some valuable services such as educational television.

The wood problem is a complex ecological, timber production, and energy question. Important parts of assessment of the problem still depend on demand information--that is, the price elasticity of demand as fuelwood becomes scarcer in a locality. However, it could be, based on U. S. experience (NESP, 1979, chap. 11), that under present circumstances the growing of wood in plantations does not compete economically, either in unit cost terms or in terms of competition of financing, with food or timber projects on comparable lands. If, nevertheless, an answer is to be sought within the context of wood biomass conversion, it might be that the public goods externalities involved will dictate a push toward remote wood growing with conversion to charcoal or to more complicated pyrolysis products that can be transported cheaply to distant users.

Improved stoves for wood and charcoal burning appear to be a least cost tactic for a provisional tempering of the fuelwood and charcoal supply crisis.

Electric grids can provide an exceedingly versatile source of energy to both urban and rural environments. In some rural areas, however, other electrical alternatives or other energy sources that can perform the same functions may become increasingly competitive.

Summing up, within the framework of this study, which takes as its main criterion the supplying of domestic energy needs to the poor,[4] there exist several promising possibilities for new sources of supply, biogas in particular. Furthermore, there are difficulties but also opportunities for an increase in supply of traditional sources such as fuelwood.

----

[4]The choice of supply options cannot be made independent of the priori ties placed on the types of demand to be satisfied and hence on the question of developmental strategy. If present patterns of cooking--the

61

_____

Footnote from page 60 continued

dominant consumer of raw household energy in most developing areas--are to
be maintained, electrification strategies, for example, may be of restricted
relevance to domestic energy needs. The perceived importance of providing
fuel for cooking, versus fuel to run pumps for water to drink, or even
energy resources to improve subsistence farming, must affect the choice of
appropriate supply strategies. Even activities that are not energy intensive, such as educational television, can still have an important impact
both on economic development and on meeting basic needs in health care.
Perhaps most important, the flexibility of electricity running power saws,
grinders, and other adjuncts to basic activities in rural and poor urban
areas must be considered a possible seminal factor in satisfying needs.
Thus, basic developmental value judgments are required in choosing between
apparently distinct energy-related projects, for example, between reforestation programs and the dissemination of photovoltaic supply units.

Chapter IV

CULTURAL AND EQUITY CONSTRAINTS CONDITIONING ENERGY USAGE

The preceding two chapters in this study have analyzed energy consumption patterns and supply alternatives of the poor in developing countries.
Clearly, high cost and technical problems are important obstacles to the use
of many of the newer technologies described in Chapter III which could be
used to meet the energy demands of the poor evident from Chapter II.
However, there is also evidence of a whole range of other constraints which
have inhibited the adoption of or limited the benefits from new economically
and technologically feasible energy systems in the past and which may do so
in the future, even when the prices of new technologies, at present prohi-
bitively high, fall to competitive levels. This chapter analyzes some of
these other parameters conditioning both the use and the supply of energy
by the poor in developing countries.

While not so easy to quantify or analyze as strictly technical or economic aspects, these other parameters are of interest for two related
reasons. First, unquantifiable or difficult-to-quantify costs and benefits
appear to be at least as important in assessing the value and impacts of
projects in developing countries as they are in developed areas. And
second, new energy technologies which do not directly match the energy
demands and incomes of the intended users will be adopted only with great
difficulty, if at all, no matter how lavish the energy assistance program.

The first half of this chapter analyzes some of these difficulties as
encountered in introducing new energy technologies, where conventional
measures of calories or joules of heat energy provided have not always

adequately reflected the wide range of energy and nonenergy services provided by traditional energy systems in developing countries.

The second part of this chapter examines another welfare problem in
evaluating potential project impacts, the extent to which the poor benefit
from the introduction of new energy systems. Existing patterns of income
distribution and ownership strongly condition access by the poor to energy
resources. High initial capital cost energy investments are beyond the
reach of the poor, even where they are economic; and traditional patterns of
social hierarchy may lead to control of new energy technologies or other
resources by the relatively well-off and so may limit the extent to which
the poor benefit from them and, in some cases, even increase the income gap
between rich and poor.

While data on energy consumption and supply in developing countries are
less than satisfactory, information on these cultural and income distribution constraints on meeting the energy needs of the poor of the developing
world is even sparser. These aspects of energy needs in developing
countries have rarely been the subject of field tests or pilot programs:
information has become available only incidentally to experiments with economic or technical feasibility, or even worse, after the implementation of
costly programs. Thus, much of the record this analysis reviews is of
failure. Less is known about the successes; obviously the poor have quite
easily adopted all kinds of new technologies which met their needs, from
kerosine stoves to transistor radios. Why did some technologies spread and
not others? More research is needed before a complete answer to this
question can be provided. In the meantime, this review draws on available
information in analyzing how different frameworks of preferences affect

energy use and how patterns of income distribution influence the efficiency and equity with which energy is supplied and the costs of providing new systems.

Cultural Preferences and Energy Use

Energy use in developing areas as in developed countries appears heavily conditioned by "cultural" habits or "tastes." But while traditional cultural rigidities are often cited as obstacles to change in developing societies, the real problem is quite often an inadequate valuation by analysts of non-monetary or not immediately visible amenities and disamenities associated with the introduction of new technologies.

Thus, various energy sources may meet more or less well demands for a particular type of heat, convenience, and religious or social meaning. Depending upon the framework of preferences of local populations—partially but not entirely shaped by income levels—these needs will have different priorities.[1]

---

[1] Income levels seem to be especially influential in the extent to which people are able and willing to bear risks. A reluctance to abandon habits tested by generations of use is often justified, given the framework of preferences of the local population. A new strain of wheat, for example, might be vastly more productive but not as resistant as traditional strains to drought or insect pests, which even if infrequent would be unsupportable by a poor farmer operating at the border of subsistence (M&P, 1975, p. 130). In Tanzania, where planting at a single optimal time would maximize crop yields, but rainfalls are highly variable, farmers prefer to spread planting over several weeks rather than risk losing their entire crop to drought. The "Green Revolution," which introduced high yielding varieties of grains into Asia in the 1960s, provides excellent examples of many of the cultural and equity problems of introducing new technologies in developing countries. See especially Andrew Pearse, "Technology and Peasant Production: Reflections on a Global Study," Development and Change vol. 8, no. 3 (July 1977), and the discussion in the following issue for a perceptive analysis of these problems.

Energy consumption habits may reflect an efficiency defined by local preferences. An energy system could provide numerous non-energy services--a pleasant smoky flavor in food, if charcoal is the cooking fuel, or a symbolic social center for the family, if an open fire is used (Arnold, 1978, p. 14). These traditional demands on energy systems are not only wider than "cooking" or "heating"; they can also be more specific in demanding particular energy sources for special end uses. In the Mbere tribe of Kenya, one type of wood is preferred for carrying a light from one place to another (a slow smoldering type), another for a quick light at night to tend a crying baby, another during the rainy season (one that will not become soggy and will dry out quickly), still another for the three-day slow brewing of marua, the local millet beer, and so on (Brokensha, 1978, pp. 3ff). In addition, the seemingly inefficient cooking fire may have a much higher total systems efficiency (see Chapter III, p. 22), even if only Btu outputs are counted, with embers being used for space heating, the fire for boiling water for washing, and coals for cooking.

Cooking Habits: The Case of Solar Cookers

The role of cultural preferences in energy use in cooking warrants special attention for several reasons. Cooking accounts for a large proportion of energy use by the poor, and numerous attempts have been made to improve upon the low efficiencies of traditional fuels and stoves.[2] The large element of personal and social involvement in food preparation, however, means that cultural factors play a conspicuous part in any alteration in energy use in cooking.

---

[2] An open fire is reported to have an efficiency of about 10 percent or less.

Solar cookers are the most oft-cited case of an energy assistance idea which foundered due to a lack of appreciation by energy planners of the cultural, "noneconomic" preferences of users--though, as is pointed out below, a more conventional economic reason (their relatively high price) may be sufficient explanation. A review of the history of efforts at introducing solar cookers reveals numerous possible reasons for failure.

The parabolic reflectors developed by the National Physical Laboratory of India in the early 1950s and manufactured for a short time by Deridayal Industries failed to gain acceptance, according to some reports, because they required radical departures from traditional methods of cooking (Mathur and Khanna, in Walton, 1978, p. 26). Cooking outdoors in sunlit areas sometimes necessitates being inconveniently distant from dwellings and in general can increase the exposure of food to dust, flies, birds and even monkeys, and the cook herself to the hot tropical sun. Being able to cook only in the daytime (where cooking is traditionally done before dawn or after dusk), cooking only one thing at a time, and having to adjust mirrors frequently have been cited as additional difficulties (French, 1978, p. 12; Fleuret, 1978; Ernst, 1977; Walton, 1978, p. 26). Unfamiliar methods of cooking may also appear dangerous (Arnold, 1978, p. 51).

In Mexico, the University of Wisconsin attempted over a four-year period (1958-1961) to introduce 200 metallized plastic reflectors, focusing one kilowatt on the bottom of a cooking vessel, into three rural Mexican villages. Results were mixed. Lof reports that even people who did not have enough food preferred buying kerosine to cook what food they had to using the solar cookers (Lof in Brown, 1978, p. 41). Problems reported included insufficient resistance to winds and rain, having to wear sunglasses to ward off glare, and unreliability of insolation. It has also been suggested that the existing knowledge of American energy technologies made Mexicans reluctant to adopt a less "modern" energy source (Ethan Kapstein, personal communication). On the other hand, some families used the cookers up to fourteen months, even though there was no evidence of scarcity of fuel (wood and kerosine) in the area. What limited success was achieved has been attributed by some to careful planning and long-term commitment by the University. In recognition of the importance of cultural factors in the introduction of such new cooking technologies, the use of cultural anthropologists has been recommended in such future attempts (Walton, 1978, pp. 58ff.).

In another effort to launch solar cookers in Upper Volta, 250 parabolic dish aluminum concentrators were introduced by the Danish aid group, Danchurchaid, and have by some reports been well received (Walton, 1978, p. 60). Other reports, however, have been less favorable as to their acceptance (David French, personal communication). Experiments with introducing solar cookers into villages to test their adaptability to local conditions will also reportedly be conducted by the solar energy laboratory in Bamako, Mali, although no results are as yet available (Walton, 1978, p. 60).

Improved Stoves

The introduction of more efficient stoves, using biomass or commercial fuels, has often met with problems similar to those of solar cookers--requiring unfamiliar methods of cooking and new utensils, appearing dangerous, and not matching the needs of the users. In Mauritania, for example, a government campaign to replace charcoal with cheaper kerosine in urban areas met with little success (Arnold, 1978, p. 14). Improved wood

stoves have reportedly been tested unsuccessfully in Indonesia, Guatemala,
and India, and in a rural development project in Tanzania by the World Bank
(Draper, 1976).

One approach taken has been to design more efficient stoves resembling
traditional models. A butane cooker similar to the traditional "Malagasy
stove" was introduced by the Senegalese government in 1974, with, however,
only limited success (Arnold, 1978, p. 14). Appropriate Science and Technology for Rural Application (ASTRA), in Bangalore, India, has made marginal
alterations in the chula which increase fuel efficiency as much as three
times, and is using highly visible demonstration projects in villages,
accompanied by trained staff, to introduce the new stoves (Palmedo, 1978, p.
106.) One problem with introducing improved stoves is that the initial
capital cost of a stove burning fossil fuel (kerosine, gas, or coal), which
must withstand high temperatures, is large compared with one that burns wood
and charcoals and the cost of any manufactured stove is high compared to
that of an open fire or homemade chula.

Biogas and Waste Disposal Practices

Solar cookers and improved stoves are not alone among energy sources in
potentially conflicting with established cultural practices and preferences.
Virtually any new energy source for cooking requires changes in cooking
habits--for example, electricity or biogas necessitate new stoves, and
sometimes changes in utensils or cooking habits. The production of biogas,
in particular, involves changes in cultural practices which in many regions
are as fundamental as those involved in cooking. "Psychological
inhibitions" against the use of night soil have been reported in Korea; a
reluctance to use food cooked with gas from human wastes for religious

worship and "pressure from elderly parents" to disconnect toilets from

biogas plants have been noted in some parts of India; and Muslim opposition

to the use of pig dung in generators has been cited in Indonesia (Barnett,

1978, pp. 102, 105, 116).

In South Asia, the caste system may be a particular obstacle, since its

basis is the delegation to certain groups of activities associated with dirt

and pollution. In some parts of India, for example, the bhangi--an untouch-

able caste--are responsible for herding swine along the roadsides near

villages to clean up human and other wastes. Their women are paid to gather

human excreta from latrines in the homes of the more conservative villagers,

where women in strict purdah cannot leave the house. Contact with these

wastes by members of other castes would make them polluted, in a religious

sense.[3]

Experience of ill health effects of handling human wastes may lie at

the basis of some of these reservations. A Balinese witch doctor warned,

for example, that sickness would result from using biogas plant slurry as

manure (Barnett, 1977, p. 105). While cow dung is considered to have

pleasant cleansing properties by Hindus, and is in fact used as an insec-

ticide and cleanser, human feces are known in India to be disease-ridden

(Moore, 1970, p. 285).[4] However, though the quantity of human wastes

is small compared to that produced by cattle, where cattle are scarce (in

Korea or Thailand) or for a poor family owning less than three or four

cattle, latrines attached to small marginally economic biogas plants could

---

[3] Clark D. Moore and David Eldredge, India Yesterday and Today (New
York, Bantam, 1970).

[4] However, treatment of wastes in the plant eliminates their health
hazards.

make them viable. In China, where "night soil" has traditionally been used
as fertilizer,[5] human wastes are reportedly an important source of fuel
for methane generators.

Summary

Different frameworks of "cultural" preferences have clearly played a
part in the lack of acceptance of solar cookers, more fuel-efficient stoves, and
biogas plants. These tastes or habits may define the parameters of potentially suitable energy sources--in some parts of the Sudan, for example,
where breakfast is at ten and dinner at four, solar cookers may be more
culturally appropriate than in India. Where cow dung is traditionally used
as a fuel, as in India, methane digesters based on animal wastes have been
an obvious choice; however, the possibilities for biogas plants using pig
wastes will probably be limited in predominately Muslim areas. In many
cases, the identification of priority energy and other needs and choice of
technologies by users could prevent the introduction of energy devices that
will not be used. In other cases, however, education has a role to play:
while the Balinese witch doctor cited above has good reason to believe that
spreading untreated human wastes on fields may spread disease, he is unaware
that the slurry from methane digesters carries no such dangers if properly
treated.

However, it is not clear from the available evidence that "cultural"
resistance in cooking habits or use of wastes is or could be the key factor
in the acceptance of solar cookers, other more fuel-efficient cooking stoves

---

[5]Eighty-five percent of China's cultivated land is reportedly
treated with organic manures, much of it human (Barnett, 1978, p. 15).

and biogas plants. Cost and the relative abundance of alternative fuel sources appear to have been at least as important as cultural preferences in the failure of some solar cooker experiments, and possibly with biogas as well (see following section). Chapter III of this study suggests that widespread commercialization (rather than gifts) of solar cookers or more efficient stoves for the poor would require drastic decreases in their initial capital costs, even if cultural constraints are not crucial. [6] Solar cookers may compete economically with other forms of energy only in areas such as Ouagadougou, Upper Volta, where fuel is very scarce and expensive; in such cases, cooking customs could change in response to economic incentives. However, measures to make energy devices more convenient or acceptable--such as storage of energy from solar cookers to allow indoor or nighttime cooking--may also increase their costs.

If costs can be reduced, the adaptability of traditional peoples to demonstrably superior ways of performing tasks and their response to economic and other incentives should not be underestimated. For example, private bank surveys in India of reasons for purchasing biogas plants have found that the clean burning gas was preferred for cooking to the smoky flame given off by cow dung, which blackens the kitchen, utensils, and clothing, and can produce serious eye infections (Barnett, 1978, p. 115). On the other hand, people in developing countries are likely to be no more willing than those in developed areas to change habits they enjoy or find convenient in order to conserve energy or use it more efficiently. The real problem

---

[6] On the other hand, environmental or social reasons may justify free or subsidized distribution of more energy-efficient equipment, in which case the cultural aspect might require primary attention. However, the possibility exists that free devices may appear to the users to have no value and therefore not be used, as has sometimes occurred in the case of contraceptives.

unfortunately may often have been that the new energy sources in question have indeed not been demonstrably superior, given the framework of preferences of local populations in developing countries.

Income Distribution and Equity in Energy Supply

Existing income distributions and patterns of ownership strongly condition the use of energy resources and the introduction of new systems. Poor people consume less energy, just as they consume less of other resources, because of their low incomes.[7] However, the question analyzed here is whether energy assistance designed to help the poor has indeed done so. First of all, high cost energy sources, even including energy investments that would be "economic" in the long term, may be beyond the reach of low-income persons; and secondly, ownership or control over energy-producing resources by the relatively wealthy may prevent the poor from reaping benefits from even heavily subsidized projects, increasing the income gap between rich and poor still further.

High Cost Energy Sources and the Poor

Some energy technologies, while within the reach of some income groups, may simply be too expensive in any sense for the poor to afford. In other cases, by using life cycle costing, poor consumers might actually be able to reduce their total energy expenditures in the long run by purchasing a more energy efficient device, but are unable to do so because of the high initial cost of the investment (even though later costs might be very small). Rural

---

[7]A relevant question, though beyond the scope of this study, is whether some energy sources are inherently inequitable or discrimatory. See for example, Amory B. Lovins, Soft Energy Paths: Towards a Durable Peace (Cambridge, Mass., Ballinger, 1977).

electrification appears to be an example of the former, while new renewable energy technologies may exemplify the latter problem.

Rural Electrification. The introduction of electricity in developing countries illustrates particularly well the limitations of an exceedingly flexible but relatively expensive energy source in meeting household consumption needs of low income people. Most countries have viewed electrification both as a stimulus for irrigation or other agricultural or industrial development, and as a means of raising the standard of living of the masses of people in rural areas (Turvey, 1978). Yet even where subsidized, electricity has not generally proven a suitably inexpensive energy source for household consumption by the poor, in rural areas in particular, since marginal costs of hookups and electricity are high due to the dispersed and small scale nature of demand.

The World Bank has estimated that 23 percent of the village-rural population in Latin America, 15 percent in Asia, and 4 percent in Africa south of the Sahara—or about 12 percent of the rural population of the poor countries—were "served" by electricity in 1971 (WB-E, 1975, p. 18). But fewer small villages were electrified than larger, and only a small percentage of the populations of the villages "served" actually had hookups. Only 25 percent of the villages in Mexico with populations of less than 1,000—where over 50 percent of the rural population live—are electrified (WB-E, 1975, p. 23). And the 40 to 50 percent Mexicans who live in rural areas consume only 2 percent of the total electricity generated in the country (M&P, 1975, p. 49). Only 11 percent of Indian villages of under 500 people, where 25 percent of the population lives, are planned to be electrified by 1985. Reddy (1978, p. 32) estimates that only about 10 percent of the

people in most electrified villages actually have electric hookups, and
Smith (1976) reports that those who do have hookups are the wealthier families and merchants.

The coverage of electricity in Latin America, where income levels are
higher, is probably considerably better overall than in Asia or Africa,
however. A study of electrification in Colombia in 1970, for example,
showed that while the likelihood of having electricity was greater for the
poor in cities than in rural areas, there was only some correlation of
access to electricity with per capita income. While 12 percent of
rural families with per capita annual incomes of $50 used electricity,
20 percent of those with incomes greater than $350 had hookups; in
small cities the probabilities were 71 and 80 percent, respectively;
and in large cities with almost complete coverage, there was virtually
the same likelihood--97 and 99 percent--that poor and rich would have
electricity (Colombia, 1978, p. 36).

Even if the poor do not use electricity directly in households, they
may still benefit indirectly as street lighting allows more nighttime activities, refrigeration in stores increases the availability of fresh produce
and cold drinks, and health clinics are able to keep medical supplies refrigerated. However, the Colombia study found that street lighting was also
somewhat correlated with income, with 70 percent of households with per
capita incomes greater than $150 having street lighting, versus 60 percent
of those with incomes of $50 per capita. Even in large cities, the respec-
tive figures are 95 and 89 percent (Colombia, 1978, p. 12).

Where incomes are very low, electricity as a consumer good, unless
heavily subsidized, is likely to be limited to a small group of the rela- -
tively well off. In that case, unless electricity is used for other,

productive purposes, load factors will remain low and marginal costs high. An Indian survey of rural electrification in 1965 showed that growth in demand in villages slowed drastically after electric hookups were installed by 20 percent of the population (M&P, 1975, p. 22). A more recent survey in Comilla, Bangladesh, where electrification began in 1963, showed that even 15 years after the introduction of electricity, less than 5 percent of the rural population used electricity. This evidence suggests that the impressive growth rates in electricity consumption of 15 to 20 percent and higher reported by the World Bank (WB-RE, 1975, pp. 24ff) may rapidly decline as expansion of the initially small base of relatively well-off consumers reaches a limit. This "saturation" level may be greater or smaller than the 20 percent reported for India, depending upon income levels, and the parameters of such a limit require further definition. The possibility of such saturation should be an important consideration in allocating new investment to the expansion of existing rural electrification facilities, to the extent that electrification is intended to meet household energy demand of the poor.

Other Energy Systems. Other new energy systems may have low operating costs but relatively high capital costs. Though the valuation of convenience and custom in such personal matters as cooking are clearly important, there were also straightforward monetary reasons--at least in India, where they were commercialized--why solar cookers have not met with success. The Ghai solar cooker introduced in India cost $14-$18 (Walton, 1978, p. 53); but the traditional chula--a kind of earthenware bucket in which wood, dung, or charcoal is burnt and a pot set on top--has virtually zero capital cost (Reddy and Prasad, 1974, p. 1481). Although the long-term operating-

plus-capital costs could possibly be lower for the Ghai cooker, life-cycle
costing is often not a practicable concept for the poor, who cannot afford
large expenditures even if fuel-use efficiency might thus be increased and
total energy costs lowered.[8]

The same appears to be true of biogas plants, which in India cost Rs
2,000 to 3,000 (about $260-$380) (Makhijani, 1977; Reddy and Prasad, 1977,
p. 1489); of more efficient stoves; and of reforestation programs, which
necessitate both an initial investment and a significant deferral (10-15
years) of the use of fuelwood (Makhijani, 1977, p. 1458).[9]

New Energy Technologies and Access to Other Resources

A second potential equity problem is that the poor may be prevented
from benefiting from new energy technologies because methods of dissemination, patterns of ownership, or local political power structures favor the

---

[8] Admittedly, applying life-cycle costing to energy investments is
difficult in practice for consumers in both rich and poor countries; the
problem faced by the poor in developing areas in making energy investments
is simply one of degree.

[9] There are important differences, however, between a capital investment
that yields an immediate return such as a biogas plant, and one that yields
deferred benefits such as a woodlot. To take a very simple example, an
investment of $300 in a biogas plant with a life of 15 years, a 10 percent
discount rate, and average yearly benefits of $50 (assuming no maintenance
or operating costs), will produce total benefits of $418 over the 15 years--
an excellent 40 percent return. On the other hand, using the same discount
rate but deferring benefits (harvesting) for 12 years, and doubling expected
annual benefits to $100, a $300 investment in a woodlot would yield discounted
benefits of only $217 after 25 years--a negative return on the investment--
and break even 44 years after the investment was made. Faster-growing species would of course affect.this result, with the break-even point at 22
years if harvesting begins after 10 years, and at 17 years if harvesting
begins after only 8 years.

(relatively) wealthy. It appears plausible that any new energy technology, introduced into unequal social structures, will be more easily taken advantage of by the wealthier and more powerful, who might thereby be able to enhance their position further. The larger farmer can afford an electric hookup, which will run his tubewell and help him to increase the productivity of his fields; he can use the dung of his cattle to produce and sell methane gas; he can grow fuelwood on his land; and he can borrow capital against these resources. The possession of capital, land and cattle allows the wealthy farmer to benefit more than the lower income population from any new technology. "Basically, it is hard to separate these groups' lack of energy from their lack of virtually every other financial and nonfinancial resource" (Palmedo, 1978, p. 98). In some cases, the condition of the poor may even be worsened by the introduction of energy sources susceptible to control by the wealthy.

Biogas. Biogas plants, for example, besides having a high capital cost, require a minimum of three to five cattle to produce the dung needed for their operation. Only wealthier farmers--perhaps 10 to 15 percent of the rural population--typically own that number (Prasad and Reddy, 1977, p. 1484). The Indian Institute of Management in Ahmedabad has reported that the average family in the State of Gujarat who owned a biogas plant also owned 10 hectares of land and 10 head of cattle; in another survey in Gujarat, the Dena Bank found the annual income of most owners of biogas plants to be $1,100 (Barnett, 1978, p. 114).[10]

---

[10] Per capita income in India was $120 in 1973. However, assuming the reference is to household income, the relevant comparison would be with a per capita income of biogas-plant-owning families of $200, given an average Indian family size of 5.5 in rural India.

Meeting the energy needs of even 10 to 15 percent of the rural population would nonetheless be a substantial accomplishment, and successful private gobar gas plants could potentially provide an efficient demonstration
incentive to small farmers to cooperate in methane generation. However,
some concern has been expressed that, as with the introduction of high-
yielding food grain varieties during the Green Revolution, only individual
rather than cooperative action will be encouraged by the success of private
biogas plants (Griffin, in Barnett, 1978, p. 70). In addition, many
wealthier farmers may prefer more "modern" fuels for cooking, such as kerosine, rather than dung, a fuel traditionally used by the poor (Pachauri,
1977, p. 132).

Further problems relating to equity involve the monetarization of goods
which were previously "free" to the poor. Livestock customarily roam freely
in India, often providing a "free"[11] source of dung for fuel to the poor who
collect it (though owners of cattle or of grazing land sometimes directly
collect the dung). This is in contrast with China, where, perhaps due to a
higher density of population, animals have traditionally been penned in community yards, one factor in the reportedly huge success with biogas there,
since collection problems are minimized (Smil, in ODC, 1978, p. IV-12).
Increased penning of cattle for methane generation by private owners in
India could even _increase_ energy costs to the poor; if dung assumes a monetary value as an input into a biogas plant, it is no longer "free" from the
point of view of the poor, who are also unable to afford the cash expenditure for the plant's output of methane gas (Makhijani, 1977, p. 1438).

---

[11]"Free" in the sense that the poor do not pay for dung in cash; but
it has a real labor cost to them, and an opportunity cost to society as
well, since the dung could potentially be used as fertilizer. However, in
areas of India where dung is not used by the poor as fuel, it is not always
used as fertilizer either.

Similar equity problems may arise with fuelwood monetarization. In some developing areas, firewood has traditionally been virtually a free good. Deforestation, privatization of land, or institutional arrangements designed to control cutting in public preserves can deprive the poor of "free"[12] (except for labor costs) wood, forcing a shift to commercial markets. In Kenya, for example, land adjudication (privatization) since 1970 has decreased the forest available to the public for cutting, as the new owners of once communal lands have gradually restricted access by others, resulting in the first market sale of firewood in 1976 (Brokensha, 1978, pp. 9ff). Commercial fuelwood plantations could have the same result.

Other Decentralized Energy Technologies. Even apparently decentralized, "controllable" technologies such as photovoltaic cells (PVCs) may be just as inacessible to the poor as is central grid electricity, since PVCs are not only very costly and capital-intensive, but are also too sophisticated to be manufactured in a developing country village (Smith, 1977a, pp. 58-59). In one project in Mauritania, for example, a solar irrigation pump introduced by the French was controlled by two well-to-do members of the village, who sold the fresh water to poorer farmers who could previously draw water from the well for free (Eckholm, 1978, p. 34ff.). In another example, while helping to create a successful village cooperative building water pumps and windmills in Tanzania, the head of the highly innovative Arusha Appropriate Technology Project admits that the group can only hope that members of the coops--only a small portion of the population of the

---

12
  If the poor gathering "free" firewood resulted in externalities, such as deforestation and erosion, then the firewood was not really "free" in a societal sense.

village, and not the poorest members--will use their new wealth to help
others (Hanlon, 1978, p. 758).[13]

Policies for Equalizing Access to Energy Resources

Low income people by definition cannot afford expensive energy systems.
Approaches that have or could be taken, however, to equalizing the access of
the poor to energy include: (1) credit policies allowing the poor to spread
expenditures over a longer period of time; and (2) technical "fixes" or
price subsidies which lower the price of energy.

---

[13]
Inequalities in access to productive resources could also affect the
ability of an entire poor nation to benefit from a new energy source. When
a large hydro site comes onstream, for example, a few large users--mines,
fertilizer plants and heavy industry, usually foreign owned--are best situated
in small countries without a national electric grid to use the large increment in cheap electricity suddenly available (ODC, 1978, p. II-45). These
foreign industries could potentially generate employment and income in the
developing country, in particular if leverage tips towards the host country
as uncertainty about the profitability of investment is reduced and
bargaining skills and operating experience are acquired [see Theodore H.
Moran, Multinational Corporations and the Politics of Dependence: Copper
in Chile (Princeton, Princeton University Press, 1974), Chapter 6)]. In the
past, however, large new industries consuming cheap electricity have not
always provided many developmental benefits, even where such projects have
been solicited by the developing country involved. In Ghana, for example,
70 percent of the cheap electricity generated by the Volta dam project--
funded by a $47 million loan in the early 1960s from the World Bank--is con-
sumed by the Kaiser-Reynolds aluminum smelter, while another, smaller hydro
project is now being built to provide more expensive electricity to growing
demand from the Ghanaian electric grid. The smelters use imported bauxite
rather than that domestically available; the total employment impact of the
projects is 0.7 percent of the industrial labor force; and exports and
imports by Kaiser-Reynolds are duty-free until 1990. Irrigation and fishing
use, once thought to be important benefits, have been limited by the government due to the severe spread of schistosomiasis in the nearby population
since the formation of the lake. Income tax revenues may partially compen-
sate for this lack of advantages, though the income tax rate is reportedly
low (Center for Development Policy, Washington, D.C., unpublished study).

Credit policies. Credit policies are one potential way to mitigate the disadvantage of the poor in purchasing high investment but low operating (fuel) cost energy-producing devices. In the past, however, credit institutions have not been accessible to the poor. In India, for example, most banks reportedly insist that a borrower who finances a methane generator have a minimum of 2 hectares of cultivable land, due to the low resale value of biogas plants (Barnett, 1977, p. 118). This could be due as much to the credit-worthiness of the user as to the economic feasibility of the project; however, in India, middle and upper income borrowers have not necessarily proven credit-worthy either--95 percent of the (subsidized) 10 year loans (mostly to the higher income groups) approved by the KVIC have been reported as defaulted (Barnett, 1977, p. 118). Since Indian banks are state-owned, this may represent an even higher "hidden" subsidy of biogas plants in India.

Both poor and rich would benefit from credit policies using life-cycle costing as a basis for loans. Life-cycle costing would take into account costs and benefits over the lifetime of a purchase in determining the credit-worthiness of a project; the high initial cost could then be spread out over the number of years that benefits will flow, with loan repayments replacing fuel expenditures. However, most agricultural development banks in developing countries--who typically fund rural energy device purchases-- have not proven sympathetic to life-cycle costing as a basis for loans.

From the borrower's point of view, the use of life-cycle costing as a basis for loans should not require subsidized interest rates, since an adequate private return exists. In other cases, however, the existence of

an adequate <u>social</u> but not private rate of return might justify subsidizing
credit or purchase of energy-using devices to take into account external
benefits to society, such as halting deforestation and erosion or saving
foreign exchange. For example, Roger Revelle has suggested that investment
in small hydro-fertilizer-forest plantation complexes at a cost of $250 per
inhabitant for the hill villages of Nepal be viewed by the Indian government
as a soil conservation measure to reduce the presently extensive flood
damage in the Ganges Plain, which would yield high social returns in India
in the long term (Revelle, in Brown, 1978, p. 24).

Technical "Fixes" and Subsidies. New technologies or technical "fixes"
may be possible in some cases to effectively lower energy prices. Energy
technologies could be made so cheap in terms of capital and material
resource input--though not necessarily labor input--that they are as
accessible to all as is the Indian <u>chula</u>. Some organizations have tried to
develop improved stoves, easily constructed by the user, for example, of
cast-off paint cans or other locally available materials; the success of
these stoves in actual use, however, is not known. In the case of woodlots,
planting fast-growing species and intercropping have been used to help offset the long payback period by providing early food or commercially salable
products such as leaves for fodder (IBRD-Forestry, 1975, p. 40). Controlled
thinning and trimming of fast-growing species for fuelwood can have the
additional benefit of accelerating the photosynthetic process and increasing
the ultimate harvest; this practice has been used successfully in Uganda and
other parts of East Africa (Earl, 1975, p. 49).

Price or credit subsidies could also be used to lower the price of
energy for the poor. Such subsidies might be considered a politically

acceptable way to redistribute income and meet equity goals; however, subsidizing energy is not the most efficient way of redistributing income.[14]
It has been pointed out that in any event subsidizing energy for the
poor is less socially important than subsidizing necessities such as water
and health benefits and that the income redistribution effect of price subsidies is relatively small in developing countries where expenditures on
electricity, for example, are typically 2 to 5 percent of total budget
expenditures (WB-Issues, 1976, pp. 56 and 45). These redistributive issues,
while certainly meriting attention, should not however be confused with the
problem posed above of inadequate access to capital by the poor despite the
presence of an adequate private or social return on the investment.

Subsidies have the additional disadvantage of often benefiting rich and
poor alike without regard to ability to pay. This appears to have been the
case in India for biogas plants, where subsidies and low interest loans have
in fact been primarily available to middle or upper class users. A survey
designed to determine motivations of biogas plant owners by the Dena Bank in
the State of Haryana reported that loan subsidies were not even important
factors in the plant owners' investment decisions (Barnett, 1977, p. 118).
Subsidizing electricity rates can have similar results, with larger and
better-off consumers or profitable commercial enterprises receiving most of

---

[14]
It can easily be shown using indifference curves analysis that the
utility of a consumer will be greater if he receives a direct income subsidy
than through an indirect subsidy which lowers the price of a single good. A
price subsidy in effect increases income; but by lowering one good's price
the policy-maker creates a bias towards the lower priced goods, thereby
inducing the user to consume more of it. A direct income subsidy on the
other hand allows the consumer himself to choose how to distribute his
increased income among goods so as to optimally meet his needs. See, for
example, M. Pauly, "Efficiency in the Provision of Consumption Subsidies,"
Kylos (1970), pp. 33-57.

the benefit of price subsidies, although such subsidies may be justified as encouraging initial use and achieving a minimum load factor. (Turvey, 1978).

Conclusion

Clearly, different frameworks of preferences affect how energy is used, and patterns of income distribution influence the equity with which energy is supplied and the costs of providing new systems. If new energy sources are to be successfully introduced or old ones more effectively utilized, these considerations should play an important role in future energy assistance programs, a role they have not played in the past. Yet, it is also evident that funds are limited and time scarce; what sort of information is necessary in order to make intelligent decisions in this area?

One guide would be to start from the apparently technically and economically feasible energy sources, as outlined in Chapter III--solar cookers in a few cases; biogas, wind and small hydro in appropriate areas, photovoltaic cells for some essential services, improved stoves, and woodlots--and try to determine the role of different frameworks of preferences and inequitable patterns of income distribution in their failures and successes, through limited pilot programs. In fact, if socioeconomic feasibility were considered as explicitly as technical and economic feasibility, both in proposed projects and in evaluations of ongoing experiments, a great deal would be added to the store of knowledge in this area.

One reason for these difficulties, however, may lie in measuring energy demand of the poor as an abstract quantity. In some cases, needs assessed by outside observation may not match present or latent priorities of intended consumers in a cultural context. The definition of energy and other demands

by local populations themselves—if feasible—would provide a more helpful
framework for considering supply alternatives. The most successful energy
technologies introduced might appear to be those requiring only marginal
alterations in current practices and institutions; for this reason, although
thus far little success has been had with this approach, more efficient stoves
that cook and look like traditional models may have more promise than solar
cookers, especially since effective cash fuel prices may be very low at present. On the other hand, clearly advantageous energy sources—such as
electricity and kerosine—appear to have had little difficulty in gaining
acceptance where they have been affordable; the factors involved in the
adoption of these new technologies should be investigated.

Existing income distributions and ownership patterns clearly influence
the benefits to the poor of new energy systems, first because even investments that are "economic" in the long-term may not be affordable to the
poor, and second, because new energy sources, like other resources such as
capital and land, are likely to be more easily taken advantage of and controlled
by the (relatively) wealthy. More careful attention needs to be paid to
mechanisms such as low cost, easy credit or subsidies that would allow the
poor to benefit from the introduction of new energy sources, particularly in
cases such as biogas in India or possibly firewood plantations where a
"free" good is monetarized as a result. While the poor will always have

less access to resources than others simply because they are poor, an impor-

tant question is whether some energy systems may be inherently inimical or

beneficial to distributional equity.[15]

---

[15]Though beyond the scope of this study, the extent to which the
poor generally benefit indirectly from productive uses of energy is an
important issue requiring further attention. Even 'if the poor do not
benefit by directly consuming new energy sources, they may still benefit
indirectly from their employment and income-creating effects. For instance,
between 26 and 80 percent of electricity used was reportedly consumed for
productive uses in rural areas of some developing countries (WB-E, 1975, pp.
24 ff.). This electricity is used in tubewells, small industries and businesses, controlled by middle-and upper-income groups--for example, 82 percent
of the electric connections in a study in Comilla, Bangladesh were to businessmen, civil servants, and farmers with more than two acres of land. If
the poor are receiving other benefits such as employment through these productive uses of electricity, this pattern of use might still be raising the
energy consumption of the poor by increasing their incomes. But Smith
(1977a) reports, based on interviews with Bangladesh researchers and their
studies, that "there is no evidence of the development-inducing effects of
rural electrification in Bangladesh although there have been monitored projects since 1963."

Chapter V

INSTITUTIONAL APPROACHES: COMMUNITY SYSTEMS

AND APPROPRIATE TECHNOLOGY RESEARCH

Previous chapters have described and analyzed patterns of energy consumption, costs of energy supply alternatives, and other social and economic
considerations in the introduction of new energy systems in developing
countries. This chapter examines selected institutional experiences in
managing some of the difficulties posed earlier in the introduction of new
energy systems for the poor in developing countries.

Numerous institutions affect the introduction of new energy technologies in developing countries. Two kinds of institutional experience,
particularly relevant to energy problems of the poor, are analyzed here.
First, cooperatively managed energy systems have often been recommended as
one solution to the lack of access by the poor to resources; the success of
past experience with community energy institutions therefore requires examination. Second, national research, educational, and technical assistance
institutions are the main link between international and national programs
of energy assistance and national policies, and the poor for whom
"appropriate" energy systems are sought; the experience of these institutions in developing countries is therefore also most instructive.

Community Energy Systems

Local energy systems may be owned and controlled by individuals or commercial firms, by local private or public cooperatives, or by state or
national governments. This review, however, concentrates on experience with

communally-owned and operated energy systems, due to their often claimed

relevance to equity problems involved in the introduction of new energy

systems.

Communally-owned energy systems have been proposed by a number of

researchers as the most efficient and equitable way to meet the energy needs

of the poor (Makhijani, 1975; French, 1978; Eckholm, 1977; Reddy, 1978;

Arnold, 1976; Revelle in Brown, 1978). Theoretically, such systems offer

several advantages. First, involvement of those who will operate the system

and benefit from it ensures that the program will necessarily be directed at

needs perceived by the community, and will continue to function with a mini-

mum of outside assistance. Secondly, the poor could contribute their labor--

previously used to "buy" "free" noncommercial energy sources by spending

time to collect them--and receive the use of a more efficient (and perhaps

cheaper in terms of labor input) energy source in return. The equity

problems involved in inegalitarian patterns of ownership and income distri-

bution, discussed in the previous section, may thus possibly be reduced.

Third, economies of scale and various other efficiencies could also reduce

costs.[1] In addition, a cooperative system might provide energy for

labor intensive village industries that would also employ the poor, and

energy for increasing agricultural production. Considerable organizational

and institutional capacities, however, are essential to the success of such

systems.

---

[1]This advantage would not accrue solely to large communally-owned
systems, of course, but to any large energy enterprise with constant or
increasing returns to scale. "Transaction costs," as pointed out later, may
even offset these economies in cooperatives.

Large Scale Biogas Systems

Community biogas systems have perhaps received the most enthusiastic attention, particularly in India. Large biogas plants should have economies of scale in capital costs, while having smaller heat losses, requiring less precision in temperature maintenance and feeding, and permitting design modifications to improve efficiency more easily than small plants (Barnett, 1978, p. 43). Whereas small private biogas plants only use the dung of the owners' (minimum of three) cows, a village plant would use the dung of every cow owned in the village (Makhijani, 1977, p. 1458). Makhijani and Poole (1975) cost out village biogas plants and conclude they are economically competitive with costs of diesel or central grid electricity generation in Third World villages. Such a system could theoretically provide employment through labor-intensive dung collection and by-product (fertilizer) distribution, increased agricultural output due both to the added fertilizer and--if the methane were used for electricity generation--to irrigation with pumps; fuel for cooking; and, again if electricity were generated, lighting, refrigeration, and energy for village industries. Small-scale industries suggested as suitable for using biogas include cement production in vertical shaft kilns; artisan and potter crafts using new foundry and glazing techniques available with gas; and even small-scale chemical and metallurgical industries which use natural gas processes (Reddy and Prasad in ASCI, 1977, p. 73).

In spite of these high expectations for community and large-scale biogas plants, the experience has been limited, but a number of new projects are just beginning or are planned in the near future. Despite generous

subsidies available for community biogas plants in India,[2] until
recently only one has reportedly existed, in the State of Maharashtra between 1969 and 1970. Three digesters were fed by public toilets and lit two
city streets; the project's termination was attributed, not surprisingly, to
transfer of the key operators and electrification of the village. More
recently, a project sponsored by the Rural Electrification Corporation in
India is underway in Karimnagar (Andhra Pradesh). The $125m^3$ plant is
planned to be fueled by 300 cattle and supply gas to thirty families, as
well as run five 3.5 Kw pumps. This plant will be administered by the
village and employ two laborers (Barnett, 1978, p. 99).

Also in India, a UNICEF-sponsored project is being developed near
Etawah (U.P.) by the Planning Research and Action Division, U.P. State
Planning Institute. It will feature two Khadi-type plants, one $25m^3$ and
one $40m,^3$ in order to assure gas pressure at all points of use, and will
supply gas and electricity to twenty-seven families (Ghate, 1978). A third
project is being carried out as a private enterprise in Valvod (Gujarat):
it features an $85m^3$ plant supplying twenty houses from sixty owned
cattle plus purchased wastes (Srinivasam, 1979).

Finally, a community plant is reported planned by the KVIC in Digras,
Maharashtra. The Digras system will charge families one rupee a month to
use ten community toilets, which together with twenty cattle will fuel the
plant. The gas will be sold back to the families, and the slurry returned
proportionately to the owners of the cows.

-----

[2]Until 1973 the KVIC gave grants of 50 to 70 percent of the cost of
a plant to institutions, 100 percent for "backward" areas. Subsidies of some
kind to community plants are expected to continue, though those to individual plants are being reduced (Barnett, 1978, p. 100).

Three large-scale plants associated with commercial activities already exist in India. The VSF Cooperative, KCP Sugar Factory, in Vuyuru, Andhra Pradesh, operates a $35m^3$ plant using dung from seventy buffalo and calves and ten baskets of sugar press mud daily. The plant cost $2,000, of which 25 percent was funded by a government grant, and provides gas to fourteen families for three hours a day at a monthly price of $2.25. Subramanian (in Barnett, 1978) reports that the plant is considered uneconomic. A second $14m^3$ facility at Madhavaram Dairy in Madras serves seven homes for eleven hours a day for $1.75 a month, and employs a full-time laborer. The third, a $70m^3$ plant serving forty families twenty-four hours a day February through July (fourteen hours a day in the winter) uses 1,600 kg of dung a day supplied by 200 cattle (Barnett, 1978, p. 100).

In Korea, a 40-family, $155m^3$ methane generator reportedly exists in Suweon, with eight more village units planned (Barnett, 1978). And a commercial pig farm, Maya Farms, in the Philippines, is probably the largest biogas facility in the world, with forty-eight $25m^3$ batch plants that are fed more than 5 tons of dung a day from 7,500 pigs. The gas is used in a canteen, a meat processing plant, a soup cannery, and to run a water pump and four freezers. A major incentive to generate biogas in this case was apparently to dispose safely of the enormous quantity of wastes generated by a large pig farm (Barnett, 1978, pp. 101 and 103).

Large-scale biogas plants operated to date appear primarily to have been associated with commercial or state-sponsored institutions. Both the organization and technical problems of establishing and running either private or cooperative biogas systems are formidable, however, and it is in any event difficult to tell from these reports how these problems have been resolved. In India and other countries cow dung has competing uses as domestic fuel, in rural house construction and as fertilizer. Raw materials must be collected and the plant maintained and repaired. Ofttimes scarce water supplies must be allocated to the plant, space for the plant and slurry drying pits located, and capital and labor inputs valued. If cattle are moved away from a village in the summer, a transport system for the wastes must be devised (Barnett, 1978, p. 116).

An inexpensive but effective distribution system for the methane and by-products would also be needed. Without a system for storing pressurized gas, involving additional expense, there would probably be surpluses of gas at some times which would have to be utilized in some mutually agreed way in a cooperative; and shortages of gas might exist at other times, necessitating a cooperatively agreed-upon rationing scheme (Parikh, 1979, p. 113).

It has been suggested that ujamaa villages in Tanzania, where collectivism is already established, would lend themselves readily to communal biogas systems (Brown and Howe, 1978). In communal China, village biogas systems had reportedly enjoyed considerable success, although factors such as simple design, government training and technical support, and traditional penning of animals may have been more important than the prior existence of collective village institutions (Goldemburg, in ODC, 1978, p. IV-12).

Fuelwood Management Systems

Forests, plantations and village woodlots can also be owned and managed privately or cooperatively, with community management again potentially allowing the poor to substitute their labor for cash. Most experience in this area has been with growing timber on public lands for commercial uses rather than to meet local fuelwood demand, though both the World

Bank and the U. N. Food and Agricultural Organization have recently shifted their emphases towards the latter, and results from some fuelwood projects are becoming available.

Multiple Product Forestry. The commercially-aimed Forest Department timber management systems of most interest here are those in which multiple products have been produced, since this practice could reduce the costs and increase the benefits of fuelwood production. Perhaps the oldest of these systems is known as "taungya," first used in Burma in 1856 to plant trees on public lands by allowing land-hungry farmers to intercrop on the land in return for caring for these trees. Variations of this system are still used throughout Asia (FAO-LCD, 1978, p. 43). A similar arrangement, the "shamba" system, is practiced in state-owned forests in Kenya:

> The main difference between the "shamba" system and many "taungya" systems is the considerable integration of the cultivators into the Forest Department. Under the 'shamba' system as organized in the 1960s the resident workman agreed to work for the forest department for nine months each year, to clear on his own time the low value cut over indigenous bush cover from a specific area of land (0.4 - 0.8 ha) each year, to allow the Forest Department to plant trees in the cleared land (the shamba) after 18 months, and to keep these trees weeded for 3 years. By tradition, the men carry out the initial clearing, but the subsequent 'shamba' cultivation is by women.

> The Forest Department guaranteed the resident workmen nine months of work per year, supplied a house and land for shamba cultivation, assisted in felling large unmerchantable trees during clearing, allowed the growing of annual crops (maize, potatoes, beans, peas and other vegetables) and the pasturing of 15 sheep. The resident worker's duties included nursery work, planting, weeding, pruning, house and road construction. The produce from the participant's shamba was considered as part of his emoluments. An assessment made in the 1960s showed that, depending on distance from areas of demand and the state of the market, and after providing for his family needs, the surplus agricultural produce could be worth up to 2.8 times the annual minimum agricultural wage applicable in the area (FAO-LCD, 1978, p. 75).

Still another arrangement, the "Mengo" system in Uganda, licenses fuelwood and charcoal cutters to remove less desirable (for timber production)
trees that crowd out high quality timber. The forest service saves the cost
of poisoning the lower quality trees (their previous policy) and, in addition, receives a royalty on the wood removed by the cutters (Earl, 1978, p.
71). A similar practice is followed by a Forest Department in central
India, where the royalty from licensing charcoalmakers more than covers
costs of replanting (Earl, 1978).

Village Woodlots. The most reportedly successful village woodlot
scheme has taken place in Korea, beginning in the early 1970s. In response
to shortages of fuelwood and erosion, the Government of Korea launched a
national reforesta tion drive in 1973 aimed at establishing self-sustaining
village-managed and owned fuelwood plantations throughout the country.
Probably critically, the project was integrated with an overall development
strategy known as the Saemuel Movement, designed to improve living conditions in rural areas through a self-help program. Elected Saemuel
Committees set priorities and made requests to the District and County
Committees. The villages supplied labor, and state and national forestry
institutions provided technical assistance, seedlings, fertilizers, and
equipment. A national government propaganda effort contributed to the
program, as did legislation requiring all steep land, whether publicly or
privately owned, to be afforested. By 1975, the annual planting rate was
40,000 ha (Arnold, 1978, p. 27; FAO-LCD, 1978, p. 76). However, recent
reports by some foreign observers have been mixed as to the actual extent of
local participation in the program (William Knowland, personal
communication).

India has also launched a village forestry program with 50,000 ha of fuelwood plantations annually planned--but success has been limited. Reportedly, local panchayats (councils) are unwilling to pursue long-term forestry goals rather than short-term needs, and the government has not provided the necessary inputs and planning (FAO-LCD, 1978, p. 70). In south-central Niger, six village councils have upon the advice of forestry officials transferred land from agricultural to fuelwood production since 1974; the goal for the early 1980s is for 70 villages in Niger to have woodlots (WB-F, 1978, p. 22). Results of this program have yet to be evaluated.

Interestingly, traditional institutions have in some instances successfully managed wooded "commons" for sustained fuelwood production. In Thailand, mangrove forests have been managed for charcoal production by traditional groups for many years; and in central India, tribal customs and practices have been used by the local people to control exploitation of forests for fuelwood (Arnold, 1978, p. 22). Where such traditions exist, the need for government assistance could be less, though rising population pressures or changing ownership patterns may eventually tax the capacities of traditional institutions. In Kenya until the 1970s, for example, some land was being privatized at about the same time as firewood shortages were becoming apparent. This could account for the lack of conservation measures undertaken by the community, despite the fact that all land had been traditionally considered common for firewood gathering purposes. (Brokensha, 1978).

Employment Linkages. Another important aspect of fuelwood and charcoal production (and forest production in general) is their employment and income-creating developmental linkages. The poor can exchange their labor

for fuel, raw materials can be provided for a charcoal industry, and charcoal or fuelwood can be "exported" to cities or to an industry to increase
local incomes. Fuelwood is most efficiently produced labor-intensively
(although charcoal production using labor-intensive methods may be
inefficient), and skills required are simple and well known in rural areas
(Earl, 1975, p. 78). In addition, fuelwood production is often located in
poorer, agriculturally marginal areas of countries, and wood is collected
for sale by the poorest, landless, and jobless people (Sivaraman, in Arnold,
1978, p. 16). In the Mbere tribe of Kenya, until recently, selling firewood
was even regarded as a sign of poverty (Brokensha, 1978, p. 11). In a plantation, wages are often 80 percent of total costs (excluding land) and those
employed are typically the lowest 40 percent of wage earners. Forest production also stimulates expansion of service industries and transportation
systems (WB-F, 1975, p. 29). For all of these reasons, positive employment
impacts on the poor of the introduction of private, state, or communally
owned fuelwood plantations are apt to be greater than on other income
groups.

Arnold (1978, Table 7) estimates annual rural employment in supplying
wood fuels to urban African markets in the mid-1970s at 246,000 man-days for
Bamako, Mali; 325,000 man-days for Ougadougou, Upper Volta; 6,000 families
for Maputo, Mozambique, and 45,000 persons for cities in Ghana. Near
Mysore, India, the Forest Department has replanted forests as plantations,
and licenses charcoalmakers to cut wood: the 5,000 persons employed in the
charcoal industry supply a blast furnace industry with 40,000 tons of
charcoal a year (Earl, 1975, p. 99). In Kenya, iron ore has been smelted
domestically and thus transformed into a more valuable product, rather than

exported, due to the availability of charcoal from the country's forests
(Earl, 1975, p. 80). Other experience and successes have been reported in
using fuelwood or village forestry projects to aid economic development in
India, the Republic of Korea, Thailand, China, Kenya, Nigeria, and Brazil
(French, 1978a; Eckholm, 1975; Arnold, 1978; Earl, 1975).

Constraints. Numerous difficulties exist, however, in the establish-
ment of commercial fuelwood plantations or village woodlots. Plantations
may not be able to cover their costs through sales, since fuelwood is traditionally considered a free or nearly free good by villagers. Even in
managed public forests, the difficulties are significant, partly because
forest services have usually allowed free or very cheap wood-gathering. In
Nepal, the Forest Service charges local people only 15 cents but outsiders
50 cents for a bullock cartload of wood (Earl, 1975, p. 82). Even the organized exchange of labor for fuelwood in a village system, or a modest
payment in cash, might seem too high a price if wood could still be
collected free elsewhere (even if the "capital stock" of the forest were
being rapidly drawn down). One study in northern Nigeria found that villagers would be willing to travel twice as far to obtain fuelwood from
existing forests at half the break-even price of a commercial plantation,
and three times as far for free fuelwood (Ferguson, in Arnold, 1978, p. 26).
A partial approach to this problem is the gradual monetarization of wood,
experimented with in some projects by initially charging prices only for
products such as timber and poles for building, which were previously
"imported" into the area and were already being paid for in money (Arnold,
1976, p. 16).

Alternative energy supplies would also have to be available if present
forests are to be maintained during the 5 or 10 years necessary to bring a

newly-planted plantation to harvest; otherwise premature cutting or poaching
by the poor is likely (Makhijani, 1975, p. 70). In China in the early 1960s,
peasants were only allowed to harvest dead trees for fuel, as a conservation
measure; this reportedly resulted in trees being stolen for fuel as soon as
they were planted, and overpruning and mistreatment of trees to encourage
their early mortality (Richardson, in Mahkijani, 1975, p. 30).

Finally, traditional patterns of land ownership or tenure might make
communal woodlots difficult or infeasible (Arnold, 1976, p. 15). Tribal patterns of land usage in Africa often do not allow setting land aside for
long periods (FAO-LCD, 1978, p. 14). Privately owned land could still be
publicly controlled; in the Korean scheme, in villages where only private
land was available for fuelwood production, owners were given a 10 percent
return, while the village controlled and managed the project (Arnold, 1978,
p. 27). In other cases where land is scarce, trees can be planted along
boundaries and roads, intercropped with cash crops or in grazing land, and
planted in marginal lands. Eighty thousand km of row plantations have been
planted in the Punjab and Haryana of India (Arnold, 1976, p. 14 ff). In
parts of Ethiopia, Tanzania, and Nigeria, communities with firewood shortages have designated agriculturally marginal lands, such as hill tops and
slopes, for forest plantings (FAO-LCD, 1978). But such schemes require more
complex management: row plantations need more cultivation and protection
than do traditional blocks; and marginal areas may require sophisticated
planting techniques, such as deep plowing for arid land, and terracing for
steep hills (FAO-LCD, 1978, p. 13).

Other Community Energy Systems

Other energy systems may also lend themselves to community ownership
and operation. A Peruvian village in the Andes, for example, has reportedly

borrowed from the national government to buy its own generators for a small

hydroelectric project, using turbines that had been installed thirty years

earlier by a group of missionaries.   Electricity is purchased by the villa-

gers with their labor in building and maintaining transmission lines, and

the loan is to be repaid by grinding the grain of other villages with

surplus electricity (ODC, 1978). Community-owned small hydroelectric-

industrial plants, together with forest plantations, have also been

suggested for the hill villages of Nepal, where Revelle (in Brown, 1978, p.

21 ff.) has estimated that a total investment of about $60,000 (or $250 per

inhabitant) could meet the energy needs of a village and increase agri-

cultural productivity. Theoretically, this could allow the marginal,

steeper terraces now being used for agriculture--and responsible for most of

the severe erosion and landslides in Nepal--to be abandoned. An equity

problem might arise, however, since the marginal land which would have to be

abandoned in order to decrease erosion is probably that cultivated by the

poor, and land reform might be necessary to benefit the poor in such a

scheme (Revelle, in Brown, 1978, p. 21 ff; Asia Society, 1978). An even

more severe difficulty could be how this $250 per inhabitant investment

might feasibly be mobilized for this project in Nepal, which had a per

capita income of $90 in 1973.

Appropriate Technology Research and Assistance

Energy research is a very expensive and time consuming task tradi-

tionally reserved to advanced industrial countries. Proven technologies

have usually been adopted later by developing countries. However, these

industrial country technologies have been criticized as inappropriate and

too expensive for many developing countries, especially for the poor.

As a result, research on energy by developing country institutions has attempted both to develop new supply technologies using available national resources, such as dung or sugar cane, and to adapt known technologies to indigenous conditions and incomes.

As implementation difficulties such as those discussed in Chapter IV have become increasingly recognized, some research institutions in developing countries have paid more attention to "propaganda"--educating people on the advantages of new technologies and the costs of current practices-- and to technical support--training operators, providing simple low cost designs and financing and/or manufacturing necessary accessories, and maintenance. Applied research, and technical assistance merge in this approach, which seeks both to develop or adapt "appropriate technologies" (in a broad sense) to local conditions, and to adapt local people to new technologies through training and propaganda.

Since research, education, and technical aid are among the variables most amenable to change in the introduction of new energy sources, how these problems have been approached by institutions in the past is of particular interest for future programs of energy assistance. A few such institutions, out of the many throughout the world, are examined below.

Biogas

India. Pioneering research on the theoretical operation of methane digesters began in India in the early 1940s under the auspices of the Indian Agricultural Research Institute of New Delhi. Government and private organizations continued biogas research, and by the late 1950s several institutions, including the Khadi and Village Industries Commission of India, the Planning Research and Action Institute (Lucknow), and the Gobar Gas

Research Station of Etawah, were engaged in promotion, field testing, and design modification of methane plants (Singh, 1974, pp. 13 ff). In the State of Haryana, 12,000 plants were installed within two years in the 1970s using an intensive media campaign, local planning and implementation, and easy credit. "Approved supervisors"--artisans trained and supervised by the KVIC as its agents--played an important role in facilitating sales, credit, construction, and technical advice (Barnett, 1978, p. 117); sales agents on commission (200 rupees/plant) are now being used by the KVIC. Under the pressures of the oil crisis, priority government attention has been given to biogas, and installations have mushroomed at a rate of 15 to 20 thousand per year.

Nevertheless, the need for a cheaper, simpler design and for better organization of technical support and training of operators have been repeatedly cited as major obstacles to the wider use of biogas plants in India (Pachauri, 1977, p. 132; Prasad, Prasad, and Reddy, 1974, p. 1353; Palmedo, 1978, p. 105; M&P, 1975, p. 106). A large percentage of biogas plants installed in India are reportedly not in operation or are operating considerably below capacity due to these factors (Pachauri, 1977, p. 101). Mardon (in Barnett, 1978, p. 98) reports that plant failures surveyed in his Indian study were due primarily to masonry construction defects, failure to paint gas holders annually, improper feeding, "lethargy of plant owners," and changes of ownership. Another Indian study found maintenance of plants generally very poor, resulting in their low utilization (Pachauri, in ASCI, 1976, p. 4). Seventy-one percent of the plants surveyed by Moulik and Srivastava in 1975 in Gujarat experienced technical problems, and a large number were closed due to these difficulties (Barnett, 1978, p. 72). These reports indicate the need for further consideration to be given by the KVIC to maintenance extension services as part of the current drive to complete 100,000 plants by 1980.

China. The reported success of the Chinese experience with biogas is said to have been largely due to the capacity of national institutions to provide simple designs using fixed concrete gasholders, mass training of technicians and propaganda. In Szechwan alone, 2.8 million peasant families are reported to use biogas, and more than 100,000 technicians have been trained. The Chinese Academy of Science and the Ministry of Agriculture and Forestry hold national conferences and local meetings on biogas, supported by applied research at local universities. Stoves and lamps designed to use methane, pipes and pressure gauges for building digesters, and designs for different fermentation pits have reportedly been developed and mass manufactured. The "ten advantages of biogas"[3]--have been widely propagandized (Smil, 1977; Smil, 1976a; Smil, 1976, pp. 102 ff). One opinion, however, is that the Chinese village tradition of keeping livestock in communal yards, rather than the alleged effectiveness of institutions, is a major factor responsible for the reported success of biogas in China (Goldemberg in ODC, 1978, p. IV-12). And curiously, at least one Western visitor found that Chinese energy experts viewed biogas as an inferior and transitional technology which will be replaced as soon as convenient by other fuel sources

---

[3]"Fossil fuel savings, reduced labor force, savings in fuelwood and grasses, straw and other crop residues can be used for animal fodder and bedding, reduced fuel expenditure by individuals and communes, less household labor for women, improved hygenic conditions of rural areas, conservation of forests and timber, mechanization of some processing tasks and local generation of electricity and less gap between the standard of living in cities and villages" (Smil, 1977, p. 27).

(Harry Perry, personal communication). This view of some technologies as "inferior" and others as "modern" is not limited to China and is quite important in the introduction of new energy systems. Though beyond the scope of this study, this topic clearly needs further investigation.

Pakistan. The Appropriate Technology Development Organization (ATDO) of Pakistan has also been involved with biogas. ATDO's approach is reportedly to select technologies developed by other institutions and subject them to field tests to determine their technical and economic viability, and social acceptability. Those that appear clearly feasible are then promoted through an extension program. Once feasibility has been established by ATDO, commercial banks are reportedly willing to finance loans (ATDO, 1977, p. 4 ff).

ATDO energy programs which have reached the extension stage include water turbines, windmills, and biogas plants (ATDO, 1978, pp. 7 ff). The precise number of installations, the actual extent of commercial banks' participation, and the success in operation of facilities are not entirely clear from the ATDO progress report, however, which is somewhat promotional in nature.

According to ATDO, the Indian-designed "gobar" gas plant with a steel gas holder proved unsuitable due to its cost and the fact that it had to be carried from factories to rural areas. The Chinese version, of brick with a relatively light cement dome, could be constructed by villagers using simple technical skills and primarily local materials, and has reportedly been successfully introduced in a number of areas in Pakistan.[4] Commercial banks

---

[4]However, the political relationships among Pakistan, India and China should also perhaps be taken into consideration in evaluating these reports.

have financed plants, and their branches are being used as "technical knowledge-dispensing centers." In a program similar to that of India, State funds have been directed at financing model plants; at a "motivation campaign," including instruction books and drawings; and, as an experiment, for two "Motivator Agents," who receive Rs.100 for each plant they help establish and operate (ATDO, 1977, pp. 11 ff).

Rural Development Institutions

Las Gaviotas, Colombia. Las Gaviotas, an autonomous Columbian govern-ment agency, has the objective of settling the frontier Orinoquia region without upsetting the ecology of the area--which has very poor soils and could not support cut-and-burn type agriculture--and by making maximum use of local resources. The strategy is one of dispersed settlement and cattle grazing, factories to process forest products, and enough agriculture for self-sufficiency in food production. Known as an "integrated rural develop-ment center," Las Gaviotas will provide central services to the region, of which the most relevant to this study is the development of "appropriate technologies" for use in the region.

Under a formal agreement with the Universidad de los Andes at Bogota, university professors and a selected group of engineering students reside for a period at Gaviotas and build a first prototype of a device based on their analysis of the settlers' needs. Then, back in Bogota, a second pro-totype is built with the added input of the University's laboratories, com-puters, and personnel. This second model is sent back to Gaviotas for field testing, and improvements are made by the original engineering group. Eventually, after progressive refinement, the device enters industrial pro-duction.

Products which have reached this production stage in the five years since the program began include a microturbine for electricity generation ($150), a hand-operated induction pump using subsurface water for homes and cattle ($15), a water ram to raise water automatically from a stream ($20), and a solar water heater ($300). The goal of technical development at Las Gaviotas has reportedly been simple solutions (but with a very sophisticated research input), high reliability, and low operating and unit costs. According to the Gaviotas philosophy, reliable and simple operation, mass industrial production, and low unit cost are more important than for the operator to be able to build and understand the workings of equipment. The relatively low unit cost of the equipment, however, is due both to the nonprofit character of the planned production and to the zero costs of technical development, since the professional time involved was donated upon condition of the designs being used for nonprofit manufacture (Chavez, 1978?). This time is of course a societal expenditure of resources, so the technical development costs are not really zero. In fact, Las Gaviotas personnel have emphasized this aspect of their project in citing the probably limited applicability of their model to other developing country situations.

Tanzania. The Arusha Appropriate Technology Project (AATP) in Tanzania has reportedly taken a quite different approach to research. Their technique is to identify suitable villages for the introduction of an "appropriate technology" and meet with a village committee to determine if the village is interested. If so, the committee appoints a survey team of members of the village, who are instructed by AATP in survey techniques and carry out an informal survey of needs. A general meeting of the village then approves their suggestions. In fourteen villages, AATP has trained

locally selected people in pump-making, and a successful cooperative has

been established which sells pumps to the Tanzanian Water Ministry. In

other in-village experiments, a methane generator that reportedly costs

$117[5] and a windmill have been developed.

The difficulties encountered by AATP in the introduction of these tech-

nologies illuminate some of the non-technical problems encountered in the

introduction of appropriate technologies. First, in building gobar gas

plants, AATP was forced to invent successively cheaper designs—from an

Indian model for $2,078, to one based on oil drums at $345, and finally to

the unwelded even cheaper model that could be made in a village for $117—in

recognition of the low incomes in the villages. Second, a fairly elaborate

manufacturing process had to be set up for windmills, which though viewed as

"appropriate" require careful balancing and accuracy. Third, the water

pumps—"a naturally decentralized technology which cannot be monopolized"—

pose the problem that anyone with the same or more skill who has the design

could compete with the original cooperative. Thus, AATP has had to revise

its philosophy of offering help to anyone, give new entrepreneurs a six-

month head start and try to encourage the adoption of technologies other

than the water pumps by potential competitors. Finally, AATP has recognized

that it can help only those with some resources or skills, not the poorest,

and can only hope that cooperative members will help other villagers

(Hanlon, 1978, pp. 756-8).

---

[5]Assuming these are Tanzanian pounds at 7.7 shillings = 1 U.S.
dollar and 20 Tanzanian shillings = 1 pound.

Summary

This review of experience with institutions relevant to equity and cultural problems illustrates the significant difficulties involved in organizational change, despite the apparent promise of these institutional approaches for better addressing energy demands of the poor. Community management of energy systems and new breeds of "appropriate" research, educational, and technical assistance institutions nonetheless should be of significant interest to policymakers, first because these organizations directly confront the difficult and crucial problems of equity, cost, "appropriateness," and cultural acceptability analyzed in previous chapters; and secondly because such institutions constitute major routes through which national and international programs of energy assistance can implement new energy systems or approaches.

National research, educational, and technical assistance institutions described here obviously have a key role to play in the implementation of new energy programs. In this area, a prime need at the international level is the exchange of information and experience on technical and economic feasibility of models, propaganda, and educational techniques, and fundamental approaches.

Only a few community owned and operated energy systems have existed, and the record of these few appears mixed. Where traditional community management structures already exist, their use may improve the chances of success. Large scale commercial and state operated systems have begun to demonstrate the organizational, economic, and technical feasibility of such technologies, but here the question of benefits accruing to the poor through positive income and employment effects again arises. At least in the case of multiple product forestry and village woodlots, these favorable developmental impacts appear quite significant, for either private or publicly owned enterprises.

Even in a community-owned energy system, the poor are not necessarily assured of benefits in a social structure in which relatively few have access to most resources. For this reason, a sectoral attack on energy needs may fail due to its inability to address these wider welfare issues. This relationship between management and scale of energy systems and developmental objectives is a key one that has not been sufficiently defined by research and experience to date.

These are only two of a number of institutional aspects of new energy systems for the poor in developing countries that require more description and analysis. The multiple aid and credit bureaucracies that impinge upon the poor, how government policies and planning influence energy supplies and consumption, and the interaction of political and economic goals in determining policies that affect energy are also important areas for future institutional research.

Appendix A

BIBLIOGRAPHY:

ENERGY AND DEVELOPING COUNTRIES

The following bibliography on energy and developing countries has been divided into three major sections, as outlined below. Marginal notes are to references used in the text.

   I. General

       A. Global

       B. Country Studies

           1. Africa
           2. Asia
           3. Latin America

  II. Demand

       A. General

       B. Surveys

 III. Supply

       A. General

       B. Conventional Sources

       C. Renewable and Noncommercial Sources

           1. General
           2. Solar
           3. Wind
           4. Biomass
              a. general
              b. biogas
              c. wood and wood products
                  (1) firewood
                  (2) charcoal
                  (3) pyrolysis
                  (4) forestry
                  (5) wood supply and demand studies

BIBLIOGRAPHY:

ENERGY AND DEVELOPING COUNTRIES

I. GENERAL

   A. Global

      Askari, Hossein, and John T. Cummings, Oil, OECD and the Third
         World: A Vicious Triangle?, (Austin, Center for Middle
         Eastern Studies, University of Texas, 1978).

      Donovan, Hamester & Rattien, Review of Literature, Conferences
         and Programs Concerning Energy Assistance Less Developed
         Countries, report to Brookhaven National Laboratories
         (Washington, D. C., 1977).

      Earthscan Bulletin, 10 Percy Street, London WIP ODR, Gt. Britain.

      Energy Update, Tata Energy Research Institute (Bombay House,
         24 Homi Mody Street, Bombay 400 023 INDIA).

      Friedmann, Ephrain, Financing Energy in Developing Countries,
         World Bank Reprint Series No. 27 (Washington,   D.C.,
         World Bank, 1976).

      Ganapathy, R. S., U. S. Foreign Policy for Energy Development
         in the Third World: A Concept Paper, mimeo
         (Ann Arbor, University of Michigan, December 1977).

      Gordian Associates, LDC Energy Supply/Demand Balances
         and Financing Requirements, final report to U. S.
         Department of Energy, (Washington, D. C., February 27,
         1978).

      Hayes, Denis, Energy for Development: Third World Options,
         Worldwatch Paper No. 15, (Washington, D. C., World-
         watch Institute, December 1977).

ODC   Howe, James W. & Staff, Overseas Development Council,
1978   with Romis Chatterjee, Manuel Taylor, A. G. Dastider,
         and Robert Nathans, SUNY, Stony Brook, Institute for
         Energy Research; and Jose Goldemberg, Center for
         Environmental Studies, Princeton University, Energy
         Problems of Developing Countries: Implications for
         U. S Policy, draft report to the Council on Environ-
         mental Quality (Washington, D. C., ODC, June 28, 1978).

      Howe, James W. & Staff, Overseas Development Council, Energy
         for Developing Countries, report to the Rockefeller
         Foundation (Washington, D. C., ODC, October 1978).

International Energy Agency, Organization of Economic Corporation and Development, Workshop on Energy Data of Developing Countries (Paris, December 1978).

International Institute for Environment and Development, "VIII. Energy Policies and Projects of the Multi-lateral Development Financing Institutions," Banking on the Biosphere--A Study of the Environmental Procedures and Practices of Nine Development Financing Agencies (London, IIED, July 1978), pp. 67-84.

Kerr, Warwick E., "Problemas Energeticos em Comunidades Pequenas, un Possivel Solucao," paper, Energy and Development in the Americas, Sao Paolo, Brazil, March 12-17, 1978.

Lenth, Charles S. and Lloyd I. Rudolph, "Energy Options: Changing Views from India," Bulletin of Atomic Scientists (June 1978), pp. 6-9.

M&P   Makhijani, Arjun, with Alan Poole, Energy and Agricul-
1975   ture in the Third World, a report to the Ford Foundation Energy Project (Cambridge, Ballinger, 1975).

Martin, William F., and Frank J. T. Pinto, "Energy and Economic Growth Prospects for the Developing Countries," Workshop on Alternative Energy Strategies, Energy Supply and Demand Intergration Through the Year 2000: Global and National Studies (Cambridge, Ma., MIT Press, forthcoming).

Meier, Richard L., Sam Berman, and David Dowell, Urbanism and Energy in Developing Regimes, report to Brook-haven National Laboratory (Berkeley, University of California, March 1, 1978).

Netschert, Bruce, "Mexico--Potential Petroleum Giant," National Association of Fleet Administrators (NAFA) Bulletin (November 1978), pp. 22-36.

Nathans, Robert and Philip Palmedo, "Energy Planning & Management in LDCs: Thoughts Concerning a Conceptual Framework", mimeo (Upton, N. Y., Brookhaven National Laboratory, 1977).

PALMEDO   Palmedo, Philip F., Robert Nathans, Edward Beardsworth,
1978   and Samuel Hale, Jr., Energy Needs, Uses and Resources in Developing Countries, report to U. S. AID (Upton, N. Y., Brookhaven National Laboratory, March 1978).

Parikh, J., Energy and Development, PUN 43 (Washington, D. C., World Bank, 1975).

REDDY
1978
Reddy, "Energy Options for the Third World," Bulletin of Atomic Scientists vol. 34, no. 5 (1978), pp. 29-33.

Ridker, Ronald, ed., Changing Resource Problems of the Fourth World, Working Paper (Washington, D. C., Resources for the Future, 1976).

United Nations Environment Programme (UNEP), Review of the Impact of Production and Use of Energy on the Environment, Governing Council, Fourth Session, Nairobi, March 30-April 14, 1976 (New York, UNEP/ GC/61/ADD., 1976).

del Valle, Alfredo, "Energy Policy Making in the Third World: Issues and Tasks," paper, Encounter 78: Petroleum and Beyond (University of Western Ontario, 30 March - 1 April 1978).

Von Lazar, Arpad, "Managerial and Administrative Aspects of Energy Problems in Energy-Deficient Developing Countries: Notes on a General Planning Framework," paper, Caribbean Consultation on Energy and Agriculture (Santo Domingo, November 29 - December 1, 1978).

World Bank, "Appropriate Technology and World Bank Assistance to the Poor", mimeo (Washington, D. C., World Bank, March 28, 1978).

World Bank, On the Statistical Mapping of Urban Poverty and Employment (Washington, D. C., World Bank, 1976).

World Bank, Rural Development Sector Policy Paper (Washington, D. C., World Bank, 1975).

World Bank, Rural Enterprise and Non-Farm Employment (Washington, D. C., World Bank, January 1978).

B. Country Studies

Howe, James W., and Staff, Energy for Developing Countries, draft report to the Rockefeller Foundation (Washington D. C. Overseas Development Council, October 1977). Appendices: energy use by urban and rural poor in (only the Brazil and Ethiopia Studies are included in the final report of October 1978):

Salvador, Brazil
Nakhon Nayok, Thailand
Panama City, Panama
Ouagadougou, Upper Volta
Sahelian Village
Debarek, Ethiopia
Syabru-besi, Nepal
My Ri, Republic of Korea
Cibao, Dominican Republic
Ulithi Atoll, Micronesia
Bagabag, Philippines
Butembo, Zaire

1. Africa

Brace Research Institute, A Study of the Feasibility of Establishing a Rural Energy Centre for Demonstration Purposes in Senegal, report to UNEP (Quebec, McGill University, 1976).

Club du Sahel (CILSS), Energy in the Development Stategy of the Sahel (CILSS, October 1978).

Evaluation des energies nouvelles pour le developpement des etats africains (Paris, Ministere de la cooperation, 20 rue Monsieur, 75007 Paris, 1977).

Ezzati, Ali, Vinod Mubayi, John Lee, Philip Palmedo and Jack Allentuck, A Preliminary Assessment of the Egyptian Energy Outlook (Upton, N. Y., Brookhaven National Laboratory for the U. S. Department of Energy, March 1978).

Floor, W. M., The Energy Sector of the Sahelian Countries (The Netherlands, Ministry of Foreign Affairs, 1977).

ODC
1977
Howe, James W. and Staff, Energy for the Villages of Africa (Washington, D. C., Overseas Development Council, 1977).

Interstate Committee Against Drought in the Sahel,
    Bibliographie du Programme Propose Pour L'Equipe
    "Ecologie et Environment au Sahel," mimeo
    (Ouagadougou, Upper Volta, CILSS, 1977).

Sanderson and Porter for the World Bank, Power Sector
    Survey: Arab Republic of Egypt, Phase I: Diag-
    nostic Report and Systems Planning Diagnostic Report
    vol. I (Cairo, 1976).

United Nations Economic Commission for Africa (UNECA),
    "Appraisal of Current Energy Situation and Future
    Prospects in Africa," Second Africa Meeting on
    Energy, March 1, 1976.

_____,"Environmental Impact of Energy Development
    and Utilization in Africa," Second Africa Meet-
    ing on Energy, March 1, 1976.

World Bank, Egypt: Review of Energy Sector, (Washing-
    ton, D. C., World Bank, June 6, 1975).

2. Asia

Institute of Energy Economics, Energy Situation in
    the Asia-Pacific Region (Tokyo, IEE, 1977).

United Nations Economic and Social Commission for
    Asia and the Pacific (UNESCAP), Report of the
    Expert Working Group on the Use of Solar and
    Wind Energy (Bangkck, UNESCAP, April 20, 1076).

_____, Proceedings of the Intergovernmental Meeting
    on the Impact of the Current Energy Crisis on
    the Economy of the ESCAP Region, Energy Resources
    Development Series No. 13 (New York, United
    Nations, 1974).

_____, Proceedings of the Second Session of the Com-
    mittee on Natural Resources, Energy Resources
    Development Series No. 15 (New York, United
    Nations, 1976).

Bangladesh
C. Lotti & Associati, Meta Systems, Montreal Engineer-
    ing Company, and Snamprogetti, Bangladesh Energy
    Study, administered by Asian Development Bank
    under U. N. Development Program (1976).

Tyers, R., Energy in Rural Bangladesh, mimeo (Cam-
    bridge, Harvard Center for Population Studies,
    1976)

China

SMIL   Smil, Vaclaw, China's Energy: Achievements, Problems
1976a   and Prospects (New York, Praeger, 1976).

India
Administative Staff College of India, Hyderabad, National
      Seminar on Energy, March 5-7. 1976, Bella Vista,
      Hyderabad, India.

Bhatia, Ramesh, "Energy and Rural Development in
      India: Some Issues," Planning and Development
      of Water and Other Natural Resources, Second
      Year Progress Report vol. II, report to the
      Ford Foundation (Cambridge, Harvard University
      Center for Population Studies, 1975).

Energy Survey of India Committee Report (New Delhi,
      Government of India, 1965).

Fuel Policy Committee Report (New Delhi, Government
      of India, 1974).

Government of India, Planning Commission, Fifth
      Five Year Plan, 1974-79 (New Delhi, Controller
      of Publications, 1976).

Henderson, P. D., Economic Situation and Prospects
      for India, vol. II: The Energy Sector (Wash-
      ington, D. C., World Bank, 1974.

_____, India: The Energy Sector (Washington, D. C.,
      World Bank, 1975).

Kashkari, Chaman, Energy: Resources, Demand and
      Conservation with Special Reference to India
      (New Delhi, Tata McGraw-Hill, 1975).

Makhijani, Arjun, "Energy Policy for Rural India,"
      Economic and Political Weekly vol. XII, nos.
      33 & 34, (1977) pp. 1451-1469.

Nagarajan, R., "Energy 2000 A.D.," unpublished mimeo
      (Operations Research Group, 1975).

National Council of Applied Economic Research, Cost Benefit
      Study of Selected Rural Electrification Schemes in
      Madhya Pradesh and Uttar Pradesh, (New Delhi, NCAER,
      February 1977).

_____, Domestic Fuels in Rural India (New Delhi, NCAER,
      1965).

Operations Research Group, Baroda, Consumer Response to Rural Electrification (New Delhi, Rural Electrification Corporation of India, Oct. 1977).

Odend' hal, Stewart, "Energetics of Indian Cattle in their Environment," Human Ecology (1972).

Pachauri, R. K., Energy and Economic Development in India (New York, Praeger, 1977).

Parikh, Kirit S., "India's Fuel Needs & Options," Workshop on Energy Demand (Laxenburg, Austria, IIASA, May 22-23, 1975).

_____, Second India Studies: Energy (Delhi, Macmillan of India, 1976).

Power Economy Report (New Delhi, Government of India, 1971)

Sankar, T. L., "Alternative Development Strategies with a Low-Energy Profile for a Low GNP Per Capita Energy-Poor Country: The Case of India," in Leon Lindberg, ed., The Energy Syndrome (Lexington, MA., Lexington Books, 1977).

Korea

Bourcier, P., Growth and Prospects of the Korean Economy, Annex E - Energy (Washington, D. C., World Bank, 1977).

Nepal

Energy Research & Development Group, Nepal: The Energy Sector (Kathmandu, Nepal, Tribhuvan University, 1976).

Pakistan

UNTI
1972
Unti, James G., The Importance of Rural Electrification in Pakistan (Washingtcn, D. C., USAID, 1972).

3. Latin America

CEPAL
1975
Comison Economica Para America Latina (CEPAL), America Latina Y Los Problemas Actuales de Energia (Mexico, Fondo de Cultura Economica, 1975).

Organizacion Latinoamericana de Energia (OLADE), Boletin
    Energetico (Quito, Ecuador, OLADE, published bi-
    monthly).

"Reports and Recommendations of Workshops Symposium on
    'Energy and Development in the Americas,' March 12-
    17, 1978," Interciencia vol. 3, no. 3 (1978),
    pp. 182-190.

Strout, Alan B., "Energy and Economic Growth in Central
    America," Annual Review of Energy vol. 2 (1977).

Brazil
GOLDEMBERG   Goldemberg, Jose, "Brazil: Energy Options and Current
1978   Outlook," Science vol. 200, no. 4338 (1978), pp.
              158-163.

_____, Coordinator, Energia No Brasil (Sao Paulo, Brasil,
    Academia de Ciencias do Estado, 1976).

Ministero de Minas e Energia, Balanco Energetico
    National (Brasilia, MME, 1977).

"Floresta--Potencial Energetico Brasiliero," Silvicultura
    special edition (December 1977).

Zoudine, Renata, and Jose Goldemberg, "Economia de
    Energia no Sector Residential," Revista do Insti-
    tuto de Pesquisas Economicas (Sao Paolo, Brazil,
    forthcoming).

Columbia
CHAVEZ   Chavez, Arturo J., "Report on Integrated Rural Develop-
1977   ment Center, 'Las Gaviotas,' Columbia," mimeo
              (Washington, World Bank, 1977?).

Chopra, S. K., An Approach to Planning and Implementing
    Rural Energy Projects, report on a pilot exercise
    in Columbia (Washington, D. C., World Bank,
    January 17, 1978).

Departamento Nacional do Planacion, Energia Rural:
    Informe del Gruppo de Energia en Areas DRI
    (Government of Colombia, December 1977).

Torres, Augusto, Stanley Lichtenstein, and Paul Spector,
    Social and Behavioral Impacts of a Technological
    Change in Colombian Villages, report to AID
    (Washington, D. C., American Institute for Re-
    search, 1968).

Jamaica

Energy Planning & Coordination Unit, Energy Sector Plan
of the Five Year Development Plan, 1978-1983
(Government of Jamaica, 1978).

Mexico

Secretaria del Patrimonia Nacional, Propuesta de
Lineaminentos de Politica Energetica (Mexico,
Comision de Energeticos, 1976).

II.   DEMAND

A.   General

Bhatia, Ramesh, "Energy Requirements of Different Farm
Systems," Indian Journal of Agricultural Economics
(July-September, 1976).

Bild, Ralph W., "Rural Energy Requirements in the Developing World," International Energy Issues (May 4, 1978).

Chatterjee, Romir and Robert Nathans, "The End-Uses of
Energy in Developing Countries: Projecting Minimal
Oil Requirements," paper, Workshop on Energy Use and
Planning in the Third World, Eastern Economics Associ-
ation, Fourth Annual Convention (Washington, D. C.,
April 28, 1978).

Frederick, Kenneth, "Energy Use and Agricultural Produc-
tion in Developing Countries," in Ronald Ridker, ed.,
Changing Resource Problems of the Fourth World,
Working Paper (Washington D. C., Resources for the
Future, 1976).

Revelle, Roger, "Energy Use in Rural India," Science vol.
192 (1976), pp. 969-975.

Somasekhara, N., "Rural Energy Structure and Pattern of
Consumption: Implications for Development Policy and
Technology Transfer," draft (Institute of Development
Studies, University of Sussex, England, 1978).

Ziberfarb, Ben-zion and G. Gerard Adams, "A Note on the
Income Elasticity of Energy Consumption in Develop-
ing Countries," paper, United Nations Conference on
Trade and Development (Philadelphia, University of
Pennsylvania, October 29, 1974).

B. Surveys

Briscoe, J., "Public Health in Rural India: The Case of
    Excreta Disposal," thesis (Cambridge, MA., Harvard
    University, 1976).

ERNST   Ernst, Elizabeth, "Fuel Consumption Among Rural Families
1977   in Upper Volta," West Africa, mimeo (Ouagadougou,
               Upper Volta, Peace Corps, July 5, 1977).

FLEURET   Fleuret, Patrick, & Anne Fleuret, "Fuelwood Use in a
1978   Peasant Community: A Tanzanian Case Study,"
               Journal of Developing Areas (in press).

Fundacao Instituto Brasileiro de Geografia e Estatistica,
    Superintendencia de Estatisticas Primarias, excerpts
    from Estudo Nacional da Despesa das Familias (Sao
    Paulo, Brazil, FIBGE, 1974).

Hackenberg, Beverly H., "Planning More Poverty: Cost and
    Consequences of Squatter Removal in Lanang District,
    Davao City," vol. 5, no. 2 (Davao City, The Philippines,
    Action Information Center, 1973).

McGranahan, Gordon, and Manuel Taylor, Urban Energy Use
    Patterns in Developing Countries: A Preliminary Study
    of Mexico City (SUNY, Stony Brook, Institute for Energy
    Research, 1977).

INDIA-   Ministry of Planning, The National Sample Survey: 25th
NATIONAL   Round, July 1970-1971, tables with notes on consumer
SAMPLE   expenditures, no. 269 (New Delhi, Government of India,
SURVEY   1975).
1975
           Musgrove, Philip, Consumer Behavior in Latin America
               (Washington, D. C., The Brookings Institution, 1978).

National Council of Applied Economic Research (NCAER),
    Demand for Energy in Eastern India (New Delhi, NCAER
    Press, 1963).

_____, Demand for Energy in India (New Delhi, NCAER,
    1966).

_____, Demand for Energy in Western India (New Delhi, NCAER,
    1965).

Sherman, Michael M., Household Use of Energy in Pakistan (Islamabad, USAID, May 1978).

Selowsky, Marcello, The Distribution of Public Services by Income Groups - A Case Study of Colombia, Part I, Electricity, Water, Sewerage (Washington, D. C., World Bank, August 17, 1976).

Wilberg, Julius A., "Consumo Brasileiro de Energia," Energia Electrica vol. 17, no. 27 (1974).

World Bank, Travel Characteristics in Cities of Developing and Developed Countries, Working Paper No. 230 (Washington, D. C., World Bank, 1976).

See also:
I. B. Country Studies.

III. SUPPLY

A. General

Arthur D. Little, Inc., An Overview of Alternative Energy Sources for LDCs, report #C-77105 to USAID (Washington, D. C., 1974)

Donovan, Hamesten, and Rattien, Inc., World Trends in Energy Supply and the Role of Inexhaustible Energy Resources in Lesser Developed Countries, and the Implications for U. S. R&D, report to the Brookhaven National Laboratory (Washington, D. C , 1977, rev. November 1977)

"Energy for Agriculture in Developing Countries," FAO Monthly Bulletin of Agriculture, Economic and Statistics vol. 25, no. 2 (1976).

Hittman Associates, Compendium of Energy-Technology-Related Assistance Programs for Less Developed Countries: Final Report, report to U. S. Department of State (Washington, D. C., 1976).

Pimental, David, et al., "Energy and Land Constraints in Food Protein Production," Science vol. 190, no. 4216 (1975), pp. 754-761.

NESP
1979
Energy in America's Future: The Choices Before Us, A study by the Staff of the RFF National Energy Strategies Project; Sam H. Schurr, Director, Joel Darmstadter, Harry Perry, William Ramsay, Milton Russell (Baltimore, Johns Hopkins Press for Resources for the Future, 1979).

United Nations Economic Commission on Africa (UNECA),
"Energy Resources in Africa," Second Africa Meeting
on Energy, March 1, 1976.

Wilson, Carroll, Project Director, Workshop on Alternative Energy Strategies, Energy: Global Prospects
1985-2000 (New York, McGraw Hill, 1977).

See also:
    I. A. Global and
    I. B. Country Studies

B. Conventional Sources

    1. Fossil Fuels

        Lambertini, Adrian, Energy and Petroleum in Non-OPEC
            Developing Countries, 1974 1980, Staff working
            Paper no. 229 (Washington, D C., World Bank,
            February 1976).

        Saito, Katrine W., An Examination of Changes in the
            Retail Price and Taxation of Petroleum Products
            in Developing Countries, July 1973-July 1974,
            draft (Washington, D. C., World Bank).

    2. Nuclear

        Ilijas, J. and I. Subki, "Nuclear Power Prospects in
            an Oil end Coal Producing Country," paper,
            International Conference on Nuclear Power and
            Its Fuel Cycle, May 2-13, 1977. Salzburg,
            Austria (Bandung, Indonesia, National Atomic
            Energy Centre).

        Strout, Alan, The Future of Nuclear Power in the
            Developing Countries, Working Paper (Boston,
            MIT Energy Laboratory, 1977).

    3. Electricity

        Munasinghe, Mohran, The Economic Costs of Electric
            Power Outages and the Optimum Level of Relia-
            bility," Report II - Outage Cost of Residential
            Consumers, Research Project no. 670-67 (Washing-
            ton, D. C., World Bank, August 1977).

        Planning Commission, Report on Evaluation of Rural
            Electrification in India (New Delhi, Government
            of India, 1965).

Selowsky, Marcello, Notes on the Appraisal of Rural
    Electrification Projects, draft (Washington,
    D. C., World Bank, 1978.

Turvey, Ralph, and Dennis Anderson, Electricity
    Economics: Essays and Case Studies (Baltimore,
    Johns Hopkins University Press for the World
    Bank, 1977).

World Bank, Cost and Benefits of Rural Electrifica-
    tion--A Case Study in El Salvador (Washington,
    D. C., World Bank, 1975).

WB-E   World Bank, Issues in Rural Electrification, report
1975   no. 517 (Washington, D. C., World Bank, 1974,
            rev. 1975).

        See also:
        I. B. Country Studies.

C. Renewable and Noncommercial Sources

    1. General

ATDO   Appropriate Technology Development Organization,
1978   Seventh Sixth Monthly Progress Report, July-
            December 1977 (Islamabad, Government of
            Pakistan, 1978).

        Allison, H. Jack, "Solar Wind, and Biogas Energy
            Systems," mimeo, report on UNEP Sri Lanka Rural
            Energy Center Development Project (Stillwater,
            Oklahoma, Oklahoma State University, 1978).

NEPAL   Asia Society, Development of Small Scale Hydroelec-
1977   tric Power and Fertilizer Production in Nepal,
            seminar, Pakhara, Nepal, February 28-March 3,
            1977 (New York, Asia Society, 1977).

BROWN   Brown, Norman, ed., Renewable Energy Resources and
1978   Rural Applications in the Developing World,
            AAA Symposium no. 6 (Boulder, Westview Press,
            1978).

        Canadian Hunger Foundation and Brace Research Insti-
            tute, A Handbook on Appropriate Technology
            Ottawa, CHF, 1976).

        Commonwealth Science Council, Seminar on Alternative
            Energy Resources and their Potential in Rural
            Development, 2 December 1976, Sri Lanka (London,
            CSC, 1977).

_____, Report on the Project Group Meeting on Alternative Energy Resources, 18-22 September 1977, Barbados (London, CSC (77) AER-1, 2 and 3 November 1977).

French, David, "Economic and Social Analysis of Renewable Energy Projects: The State of the Art," paper, USAID Africa Bureau Firewood Workshop, Washington, D. C., 12-14 June, 1978.

_____, "The Economics of Renewable Energy Systems for Developing Countries," (Washington, D.C., 4417 Q Street, NW, January 1979).

HAMMOND 1977

Hammond, Allen, "Unconventional Energy Sources: Brazil Looks for Applications," Science vol. 195 (1977), pp. 862-863.

Lawand, T A., "The Potential of Renewable Energies in Planning the Development of Rural Areas," report to the International Solar Energy Society (Quebec, Brace Research Institute, 1978).

LOVINS 1978a

Lovins, Amory B., "Soft Energy Technologies," American Review of Energy (1978) 3:477-517

National Academy of Sciences, Energy for Rural Development: Renewable Resources and Alternative Technologies for Developing Countries (Washington, D. C., NAS, 1976).

Pak, Simon J. and Charles R. H. Taylor, "Critical Factors in Economic Evaluation of Small Decentralized Energy Projects," Science and Technology Report no. 25 (Washington, World Bank, November 1976).

Reddy, A. K. N., "Non-Commercial Fuels in Developing Countries" (United Nations Environment Program, pre-print).

REDDY & PRASAD 1977

_____, and K. K. Prasad, "Technological Alternatives and the Indian Energy Crisis," Economic and Political Weekly, special issue (August 1977).

SMIL 1977

Smil, Vaclaw, "Intermediate Energy Technology in China," Bulletin of Atomic Scientists vol. 33, no. 2 (1977), pp. 25-31.

SMIL 1976

_____, "China Opts for Small-Scale Energy Technologies," Energy International (February 1976).

SMITH
1977

Smith, Douglas V., "Small-Scale Energy Activities in India and Bangladesh, Trip Report, March 17-31 and April 3-13, 1977," Working Paper no. MIT EL 77-025 WP (Boston, MIT Energy Laboratory, August 31, 1977).

Street, James H., "Economic and Social Implications of Non-Conventional Energy Use in Rural Latin America," paper, Energy and Development in The Americas, Sao Paolo, Brazil, March 12-17, 1978.

Suarez, Carlos E., "Implicaciones Sociales y Economicas del Desparollo de las Fuentes no Convencionales de Energia," paper, Energy and Development in the Americas, Sao Paolo, Brazil, March 12-17, 1978

United Nations Economic and Social Commission for Africa (UNESCA), "Geothermal Resources Potential in Africa and Recommendations for Development," Second Africa Meeting on Energy, March 1, 1976

2. Solar

Agarwal, Emil, "Solar Energy and The Third World," New Scientist vol. 77, no. 1089 (1978), pp. 357-359.

Bartlett, Melinda A., "Solar Energy for Developing Countries," paper for International Energy Issues Course (Washington, D. C., Johns Hopkins University, SAIS, April 28, 1978).

BROWN &
HOWE
1978

Brown, Norman L. and James W. Howe, "Solar Energy for Village Development" Science vol. 199 (1978), pp. 651-657.

Florida Institute of Technology, Center for Energy Alternatives, Solar Cookers for Haiti: A Feasibility Study (November 1975).

Gopalakrishman, N K., "Global Survey of Solar Energy R&D," mimeo (Urja, January 21, 1978).

GOPALAKRISHMAN
1978

Gordon, Lincoln, "Foreign Policy Aspects of U. S. Solar Energy Development," panel presentation (Washington, D. C., Commerce Department Solar Energy Conference, July 10, 1978).

Hayes, Denis, Rays of Hope (New York, W. W. Norton for Worldwatch Institute, 1977).

International Solar Energy Society, Sharing the Sun Technology in the Seventies, nine volumes (Winnipeg, ISES, August 1976).

Langford, Debra, "Solar Energy and the Developing Nations: The Role of the United States," paper for International Energy Issues course (Washington, D. C., Johns Hopkins University, SAIS, May 1978).

Lilien, Gary L., "The Diffusion of Photovoltaics: Background, Modeling and Initial Reaction of the Agricultural-Irrigation Sector," MIT Energy Laboratory Report no. 78 (Cambridge Mass., MIT, March 1978).

Makhijani, Arjun, "Solar Energy and Rural Development for the Third World," The Bulletin of the Atomic Scientists vol. 32, no. 6 (1976), pp. 14-24.

Malik, M. A. S., "Summary of International Programs in Solar Energy R&D," mimeo (Kuwait, report to the U. S. Department of Energy).

Mathur, K. N., and Khanna, M. L , "Application of Solar Energy to Small-Scale Industry," Journal of Solar Energy Science and Engineering I (1957), pp. 34-36.

Moisan, Francois and Daniel Thery, "Towards a New Industrial Vegetel Civilization--Principal Solar Programs in Brazil and Australia," Ecodevelopment News no. 3 (October 1977), pp. 29-34.

National Academy of Science, Solar Energy in Developing Countries: Prospectives and Prospects (Washington, D. C., NAS, 1972)

TANZANIA
1978
National Academy of Science and Tanzanian National Scientific Research Council, Workshop on Solar Energy for the Villages of Tanzania, Dar es Salaam, August 11-19, 1977 (Washington, D. C., NAS, 1978)

United Nations University, "Solar Energy: Immediate Important Role in Villages," UNU Newsletter vol. 2, no. 3 (no date), pp. 3-4.

"Solar Energy: Unsung Potential for Wind and Biomass" Science vol. 200 (May 12, 1978).

SMITH
1978

Smith, Douglas V., Consultant, and Stephen V. Allison, Micro Irrigation with Photovoltaics (Boston, MIT Energy Laboratory, April 1978).

_____, Photovoltaic Power in Less Developed Countries, report to ERDA (Lexington, MA., MIT Lincoln Laboratory, March 24, 1977).

T. B. Taylor Associates, A Preliminary Assessment of the Possibilities for the Worldwide Use of Solar Energy, preliminary draft report to the Rockefeller Foundation (Damascus, Maryland, February 1978).

WEISS
1976

Weiss, Charles, and Pak, Simon, Developing Country Applications of Photovoltaic Cells, mimeo (Washington, D. C., ERDA, 1976)

United Nations, Proceedings of the United Nations Conference on New Sources of Energy, vol. 5 Solar Energy: II, Rome (New York, N. Y., 1964).

United Nations Economic and Social Commission for Africa (UNESCA), "Present Status and Future Prospects for Solar Energy Utilization in Africa," Second Africa Meeting on Energy, March 1, 1976.

WALTON
1976

Walton, J. D., A. H. Roy, and S. H. Bomar, Jr., A State-of-the-Art Survey of Solar Powered Irrigation Pumps, Solar Cookers, and Wood-Burning Stoves for Use in Sub Sahara Africa, report to Al Dir'Iyyah Institute, Geneva, (Atlanta, Georgia Institute of Technology, January 1978).

de Winter, F. & J. N. de Winter, eds., Description of the Solar Energy R&D Programs in Many Nations, final report to ERDA (Santa Clara, CA., Atlas Corporation, February 1976).

3. Wind

Fraenkel, Peter L., Food from Windmills: A Report on the Windmill Irrigation Project Initiated by the American Presbyterian Mission at Omo Station in Ethiopia (London, Intermediate Technology, November 1975).

Heronemus, William E., "A Survey of the Possible
    Use of Windpower in Thailand and the
    Philippines," Report to AID/OST (1974).

Meriam, Marshall F., "Windmills for Less Developed
    Countries," Technos (April 1972).

Templin, R. J., "Wind Energy: Some Technical and
    Geographic Aspects," paper, Energy and Develop-
    ment in the Americas, Conference, Sao Paolo,
    Brazil 12-17, March 1978.

Tewari, Sharat K., "Economics of Wind Energy Use
    for Irrigation in India," Science vol. 202
    (November 3, 1978), pp. 481-486.

4. Biomass

  a. General

Acioli, Jose de Lima, "Alcool Como Combustivel--
    Desenvovimentos Recentes," paper, Energy and
    Development in the Americas, conference
    Sao Paolo, Brazil, March 12-17, 1978.

Hammon, Allen, "Biomass Conversion--A Rediscovered
    Source of Fuels," paper, Energy and Develo-
    ment in the Americas, Sao Paolo, Brazil, March
    12-17, 1978.

Poole, Alan, "Energy from Biomass: A Conceptual
    Overview," study for ERDA/APAE (Washington,
    D. C , Institute for Energy Analysis/Oak
    Ridge, September 1977)

  b. Biogas

Appropriate Technology Development Organization,
    Gobar Gas: An Alternate Way of Handling
    the Village Fuel Problem, Fertilizer and
    Fuel (Islamadad, Government of Pakistan,
    1978).

Barnett, Andrew, Leo Pyle, and S. K. Subramanian,
    Biogas Technology in the Third World: A
    Multidisciplinary Review (Ottawa, Interna-
    tional Development Research Centre, 1978).

Bhatia, Ramesh, "Economic Appraisal of Bio-Gas
    Units in India: Framework for Social Benefit
    Cost Analysis," Economic and Political Weekly
    vol. XII, nos. 33834, pp. 1503-1518.

128

Ghate, P.B., and K.K. Singh, "Action Research in Biogas Development" mimeo (Planning Research and Action Division, Uttar Pradesh, India, 1978).

McGarry, Michael G., and Jill Stainforth, Compost, Fertilizer, and Biogas Production for Human and Farm Wastes in the People's Republic of China (Ottawa, International Development Research Center, 1978).

Moulik, T. K., and U. K. Srivastava, Bio-gas Plants at the Village Level: Problems and Prospects In Gujarat (Ahmedabad, India Institute of Management, 1975).

NAS
1977

National Academy of Science, Methane Generation from Human, Animal, and Agricultural Wastes (Washington, D. C., NAS, 1977).

PRASAD,
PRASAD &
REDDY
1974

Prasad, C. R., K. K. Prasad, and A. K. N. Reddy, "Biogas Plants: Prospects, Problems and Tasks," Economic and Political Weekly, special issue (August 1974), pp. 1347-1364.

SINGH
1974

Singh, Ram Bux, Bio-Gas Plant: Generating Methane from Organic Wastes (Ajitmal, Etawah, India, Gobar Gas Research Station, 1974).

Smil, Vaclaw, "China Claims Lead in Biogas Energy Supply," Energy International (June 1974).

Solly, R. K., "A Study of Methane Digesters in the South Pacific Region," Appropriate Technology vol. 3, no. 4 (1977).

Thery, Daniel, "Biogaz: A Program for Sahelian Countries," Ecodevelopment News no. 3 (October 1977).

3. Wood and Wood Products

Firewood

Arnold, J. E. M., "Wood Energy and Rural Communities" paper, Eighth World Forestry Congress (Jakarta, Indonesia, October 16-28, 1978)

_____, "Wood for Energy," mimeo (Rome, United Nations Food and Agriculture Organization, 1976).

BROKENSHA   Brokensha, David and Bernard Riley, Forest,
1978   Foraging, Fences and Fuel in a Marginal Area of
                Kenya, USAID Africa Bureau Firewood Workshop,
                Washington, D. C., June 12-14, 1978.

                Canadian International Development Agency, "Study
                mission on forest energy in the Sahel and West
                Africa, October 2-December 17, 1974."

DEBOISEMENT   "Le Deboisement en Haute-Volta: Les Besoins en Bois
1976   de Chauffe de Ouagadoogo," Le Developement
                Voltaique no. 40 (Ouagadougou, Upper Volta,
                SAED, August 1-31, 1976).

                Digernes, Turi Hammer, Wood for Fuel--Energy Crisis
                Implying Desertification: The Case of Bara, the
                Sudan, abstract of Ph.D. dissertation (Oslo,
                Norway, Department of Geography, University of
                Bergen, July 1977)

                Draper, S. A., Wood Processing and Utilization at
                Village Level, Third FAO/SIDA Expert Consulta-
                tion on Forestry for Local Community Develop-
                ment, 1977.

                Earl, D.E., Forest Energy and Economic Development
                (Oxford, Clarendon Press, 1975).

                Eckholm, Erik, "Firewood: The Poor Man's Burden,"
                International Wildlife (May-June 1978).

                _____, The Other Energy Crisis: Firewood, World-
                watch Paper no. 1 (Washington, Worldwatch
                Institute, September 1975).

FRENCH   French, David, Firewood in Africa, AID Africa Bureau
1978   Firewood Workshop, Washington, D. C., June 12-
                14, 1978.

                von Oppen, M., "A Note on Recent Developments in the
                Prices of Fuel for Domestic Use in India," paper,
                International Seminar on Energy, Hyderabad,
                India, January 4-7, 1979.

                Openshaw, Keith, "Woodfuel, A Time for Reassessment,"
                Natural Resources Forum (1978).

                _____, La Foret Amazonienne--Source d'Energie
                (Paris, Centre Technique Forestier Tropical,
                1971).

United Nations Economic Commission on Asia and the
Pacific (UNESCAP), "Wood as a Source of Energy,"
Second Africa Meeting on Energy, March 1, 1976.

United Nations Environmental Program, Consultancy on
Firewood and Substitutes in the Sahelian Zone
and North Africa, report (Nairobi, UNEP, 1976).

Charcoal

Earl, D. E., Charcoal and Forest Management, limited
circulation (Department of Forestry, University
of Oxford, 1973).

_____, Ivory Coast-the Place of Charcoal in the
Economy, limited circulation (Abidhan, FAO/ILO,
1972)

_____, Madagascar, the Potential for Charcoal, UNDP
FO SF/NAG 8 (Rome, FAO, 1971).

_____, Nepal--The Charcoal Industry and Its Potential
Contribution to the Economy of Nepal, technical
report NEP/69/513 (Rome, FAO, 1973).

Kokwaro, J. O., "Workshop on Advantages and Disadvan-
tages of Charcoal Burning in Kenya," paper,
Workshop on Environment and Rural Development in
Africa, Kenya, November 11-30, 1974.

Uhart, Edmond, Le charbon de bois a Madagascar (Addis
Ababa, UNECA, 1976).

_____, Charcoal in the Sahelian Zone (Addis Ababa,
UNECA, 1975).

_____, Charcoal Industry in the Sudan (Addis Ababa,
UNECA, 1976)

_____, Charcoal Problem in Somalia (Addis Ababa,
UNECA, 1976).

Pyrolysis

Chiang, Tze I., John W.Tatom, J. W. S. de Graft-
Johnson, and J. W. Powell, Pyrolytic Conversion
of Agricultural Forestry Wastes in Ghana, report
to USAID (Atlanta, Georgia Institute of Technology, July 1976).

TATOM
1976

Georgia Institute of Technology with the Development
Technology Center of Bandung Institute of Tech-
nology and the University of Padjadaran,
Pyrolitic Conversion of Agricultural and Fores-
try Wastes to Alternate Energy Sources in
Indonesia--A Feasibility Study, report to AID,
February 1977 (Project A-1914, AID/ASIA-C-1203)

Forestry
Bene, J. G., et al., Trees, Food and People: Land
Management in the Tropics (Ottawa, International
Development Research Centre, 1977).

Cliff, Edward P , Utilization of Tropical Forests:
Review of the Forestry Literature in the A.I.D.
Reference Center (Washington, D. C., AID/TAB,
1973)

WB-F
1978

Donaldson, Graham, Forestry: Sector Policy Paper
(Washington, D. C., World Bank, February 1978).

DRAPER
1976

Draper, S. A., et al., Forestry Sub-Sector Report
(Washington, D. C., World Bank, 1976).

EARL
1975

Earl, D. E., "Latest Techniques in the Treatment of
Natural High Forest in South Mengo District,"
paper, 9th Commonwealth Forestry Conference
(Entebbe, Government Printer, 1968).

Frimigacci, M. Bucket, "Ecologie et Environment au
Sahel" (Ouagadougou, Comite Permanent Interetats
de Lutte Contre La Secheresse Dans Le Sahel
(CILSS), 1977).

Kernan, H S., Preliminary Report on Forestry in
Vietnam, Working Paper no. 17 (Saigon, Joint
Development Group, 1968).

King, K. F. S., Forestry and Forest Industries in
Nepal, mimeo (Washington, D. C., IBHD report,
1970).

Kingston, D., Growth Yield and Rotation of Seedling
Crops of Eucalyptus Grandis in Uganda, technical
note 193/172 (Entebbe, Uganda Forest Department,
1972).

Logan, W. E. M., "Fast-Growing Tree Species for
Industrial Plantations in Developing Countries
Unasylva vol. 19 (1965), pp. 159-167.

Moore, D., "The Effects of An Expanding Economy on the Tropical Shelterwood System in Trinidad," paper, 7th Commonwealth Forestry Conference (Port of Spain, Trinidad, Forest Department, 1957).

National Academy of Sciences, Leucaena: Promising Forage and Tree Crop for the Tropics (Washington, D. C , NAS, 1977).

National Commission on Agriculture, Interim Report on Production Forestry--Man-Made Forests (New Delhi, Government of India, 1972).

Nowak, K. and A. Polycaropou, "Sociological Problems and Asian Forestry," Unasylva vol. 23, no. 19 (1969).

Sanger, Clyde, Trees for People: An Account of the Forestry Research Program Supported by the International Development Research Centre (Ottawa, IDRC, 1977).

Sivaraman, B., "Forestry for Community Development (Village Forestry)," paper, Second FAO/SIDA Expert Consultation on Forestry for Community Development, Rome, 21-22 June 1977.

UNFAO, Forestry for Local Community Development Forestry Paper No. 7, M-36 ISBN 92-5-100586-0 (Rome, FAO, 1978).

Weber, Fred R., Reforestation in Arid Lands (Action/Peace Corps Program and Volunteers in Technical Assistance, 1977).

Webster, G., Working Plan for South Mengo Forests (Entebbe, Uganda Forest Department, 1961).

Westoby, J. C., "The Role of Forest Industries in the Attack on Economic Underdevelopment," Unasylva vol. 16 (1963), pp. 168-201.

World Bank, "Forestry and Forest Industries in Nepal," unpublished mimeo (Washington, D. C., World Bank, 1970).

Wood Supply and Demand Studies
Clark, W. F., "Timber Supply and Demand for 1970-1990," Nepal Project Report no. 1, mimeo (Rome, FAO' 1970).

Gambia Land Resources Development Project, The Gambia: A Wood Consumption Survey and Timber Trend Study 1973-2000, report to ODA (U.K.)/ LRD (London, GLRDP, 1973).

Lerche, C. and A. S. Khan, An Estimate of Timber Trends in West Pakistan (Rome FAO, 1970).

Openshaw, Keith, Present Consumption and Future Requirements of Wood in Tanzania, technical report no. 3, FO SF/Tan 15 (Rome, FAO, 1971).

Rocha, A. A., "Carvoes Brasilieros: Reservas e Utilizacao," paper, Energy and Development in the Americas, Sao Paolo, Brazil, March 12-17, 1978.

Skold, P., Present and Future Wood Demand and Supply - Kenya (Rome, FAO, 1970).

United Nations Food and Agriculture Organization, Development and Forest Resources in Asia and the Far East: Trends and Perspectives, 1961-91 (Rome, FAO, 1976).

_____, Nigeria: The Market for Firewood, Poles and Sawnwood in the Major Towns and Cities in the Savanna Region, technical report no. 6, SF/NIR 16 (Rome, FAO, 1972)

_____, Sudan: Present Wood Consumption and Future Requirements, T. A. no. 1820 (Rome, FAO, 1964).

_____, Tanzania: Present Consumption and Future Requirements of Wood in Tanzania, technical report no. 3, SF/TAN 15 and project working document (Rome, FAO, 1964).

_____, Thailand: Present and Future Forest Policy Goals, A Timber Trend Study 1970-2000, T.A. 3156 and project working document (Rome, FAO, 1972).

_____, "Wood: World Trends and Prospects," Unasylva vol. 20.

_____, World Forest Inventory 1963 (Rome, FAO, 1966).

_____, Yearbook of Forest Products, 1966-1976 (Rome, FAO, 1976).

IV. BIBLIOGRAPHIES AND LISTS OF ACTIVITIES

Arnold, J. E. M., Wood Energy and Rural Communities, paper,
    Eighth World Forestry Congress, Jakarta, Indonesia,
    16-28 October, 1978 (FAO).

Donovan, Hamester & Rattien, Inc., Review of Literature,
    Conferences and Programs Concerning Energy Assistance
    to Less Developed Countries, report to Brookhaven
    National Laboratories (Washington, D. C., December 30,
    1977). Annotated bibliography.

French, David, Economic and Social Analysis of Renewable
    Energy Projects: The State of the Art, report to
    USAID, November 22, 1977. Annotated bibliography.

_____, Firewood in Africa, paper, USAID. Africa Bureau
    Firewood Workshop, June 12-14, 1978. Annotated
    bibliography.

Smith, Douglas V., Small-Scale Energy Activities in India
    and Bangladesh-Trip Reports-March 17-31, 1977 and
    April 3-14, 1977. Energy Laboratory Working Paper
    no. MIT-EL-77-025WP (Cambridge, MA., MIT, August 31,
    1977).

Tranet (Transnational Network for Appropriate/Alternative
    Technologies), Rangeley, Maine, published quarterly,
    especially no. 7, summer 1978 (directory of people
    working in alternative energy research as it applies
    to use in LDCs).

Walton, J. D., A. H. Roy, and S. H. Boman, Jr., A State-of-
    the-Art Survey of Solar-Powered Irrigation Pumps,
    Solar Cookers, and Wood Burning Stoves for Use in Sub-
    Sahara Africa, report to the al Dir'iyyah Institute
    (Atlanta, GA., Georgia Institute of Technology, 1978).

Appendix B

OBSERVATIONS ON SOME ASPECTS OF ENERGY USE
IN CAMEROON*

by Emmanuel Mbi

The average rural dweller in Cameroon, as would be expected, uses very little marketed energy or fuels compared with the urban dweller. He relies more upon non-commercial forms for basic energy requirements. However, there is a remarkable similarity in terms of the forms of energy used by the poorest segments of the rural and urban population. The same is not exactly true of the more well-to-do segments of both the rural and the urban populations. The forms of energy or fuels that the rural well-to-do use is more similar to that of the rural and urban poor in kind but not in quantity. This could be explained in part by the role that tradition plays in determining the choice or preference for certain types of fuels, the rural areas of course being more tradition-oriented than the urban areas. Nevertheless, for a few extremely wealthy rural dwellers, there is little or no difference between them and the better-off urban dwellers in terms of the kinds of forms of energy they most rely on.

The main energy forms used in Cameroon can be classified into three general categories: (1) electricity, (2) other commercial energy, and (3) noncommercial energy.

1. Electricity

Electricity comes from three sources: (a) hydro stations, (b) diesel-run thermal power plants, and (c) small generators. The major hydro stations in the country, though only three in number, provide electricity to more places and people than the more numerous thermal plants and small generators.

---

*While the information contained here has not been used in our energy data base, this appendix is of particular interest in the light it throws on the social and cultural factors affecting household energy use.

Most of the electricity is consumed by industry, but we are here concerned mainly with non-industry energy consumption. Roughly 50-60 percent
of the urban areas are electrified; for the rural areas, a liberal estimate
would be about 10-15 percent.

Electrical connections are highly regarded by households and other
establishments. The system used is the European 200 volt, 50 cycle standard
system. Production levels relative to capacity are usually high for
electricity generated by the hydro stations (as most of industry relies on
this source) and low for the thermal plants even for urban areas with large
populations. The diesel-run thermal power plants and the hydro stations are
owned and operated by the state-owned electricity corporation while the
small generators are usually privately owned except those that are used to
electrify the homes of senior government officials as well as hospitals
in areas that do not yet have electricity.

Lighting is the foremost item that leads to demand for electricity.
When electricity is introduced into an area by the government utility, the
principal streets are first lit, then commercial buildings and then homes.
For the average home there is usually only one overhead bulb in the living
room and one each in every bedroom; no table or sidelamps. While lighting
could be said to be of foremost importance where demand for electricity is
concerned in Cameroon, the importance attached to other uses for electricity
in the household varies according to income levels.

Ventilating fans are accorded a high priority as well as electric irons
(more convenient to use than charcoal irons), followed by refrigerators,
radios and record players and air conditioners. Refrigerators are widely
desired not necessarily for food preservation but for water cooling and for
drinks (sometimes for sale). Culturally, many of the people do not like

refrigerated food. Most preserved food is either smoked or dried. Electric cookers are not very common and are not very popular even with those well-to-do who can afford them. There is a suspicion about them which is fueled by rumors of electric cookers blowing up very easily. Thus, electricity demand for cooking is almost negligible. Even families that own an electric cooker do not always use it, not because of the cost of electricity but because of that lingering suspicion: it may function as a status symbol.

What is the electricity use pattern by income levels in the urban areas? Urban centers in Cameroon can be classified under three income levels: the upper, the middle, and the lower. The upper income group is almost always made up of high government officials, businessmen, company executives; the middle income group is usually made up of middle level government officials, company workers, some businessmen and many in the informal sector. The lower income group usually comprises a great mixture of people. There are some who are extremely poor, some not so poor, newly arrived people from the village, laborers and some self-employed persons whose businesses are not doing so well.

For the upper income persons, all activities demanding electricity could be found to be in their lists of priorities. Their houses are well lit, most often have fans or air conditioners; of course they own irons, electric shavers, toasters, electric sewing machines and anything else that sets them apart from the rest. The middle income generally have as their first priority lighting, then fans, irons end then radios and for the young, record players. For the lower income people, who are actually the urban poor, usually less than 25 percent of the poor have electric light. As for the more fortunate members of the lower income group, usually some laborers and members of the informal sector who are able to go beyond just being able to afford lighting, their next priorities seem to be radios and/ or irons. Radios are valued because of the news, music and announcements of job openings, and irons because most dresses and clothes are cotton and not permanent press. Additionally, electric irons are more convenient than the charcoal box irons which are also not very clean to use. Generally, electric demand among the urban poor is very low because of the costs involved both for the electricity and for the appliances involved. In addition, the government has no program to make it affordable to that segment of the population.

Space heating is not a factor in electricity demand or consumption in Cameroon. Most of the country is warm all year round. However, there are certain areas, particularly in the mountainous regions, that get quite cold with temperatures going down as low as 35° F and heating could probably be used. Nevertheless, rooted in the tradition and culture of most of the people of Cameroon is the belief that heating a house or being unable to withstand the usually brief cool weather is a sign of weakness. In cold rural areas where open wood fires are predominant, children sitting around such fires to warm themselves are usually reprimanded by the elders. Only the aged are permitted such things.

On a community scale, aside from industrial and hospital electricity use and street lighting, water supplies use substantial amounts of electric power to pump into holding tanks and inner reservoirs. Even in areas where there is no electricity, small generators are used for that purpose.

On the average, demand for electricity is about 23 kwh/capita/month.
A user with one light bulb (75 watts), an electric fan, a radio and an iron
in 1972 paid about 500 francs a month, the cost of electricity being about
18-20 CFA francs per kwh. As of May 1977, the cost of electricity had more
than doubled to an average of 50 CFA francs per kwh end even went as high as
80 CFA francs per kwh in some areas. Eighty CFA francs is about 34 U. S.
cents. It is not quite clear why these steep price increases have taken
place. However, it is known that the sharpest increase occured in areas
whose electricity supply comes from diesel-run thermal power plants. This
fact may be attributed to the increases in the price of imported oil.

2. Other Commercial Energy

More commercial energy, by which is meant here diesel, petrol, kerosine, bottled gas, coal, spirits and aviation fuel is, of course, used for
all purposes in the urban areas than in the rural areas.

Diesel is used mainly for transport (trucks) and as earlier stated for
thermal electricity generators. Petrol is also used for transport (light
trucks, cars, and motorcycles) and since more urban dwellers than rural ones
own vehicles, the demand is certainly greater in the cities. Most of the
transportation in the country is done by land. Heavy trucks account for
most of the diesel consumption in road transport. The 1973/74 oil crisis
brought about a steep increase in the price of petroleum products with
petrol and diesel prices increasing by as high as 400-500 percent in one
year. For example, in November 1972, petrol cost 50 francs a litre, but in
April 1974, it was 250 francs a litre in certain areas and averaging 170
francs CPA in others. Public transportation (taxis, buses, trains, etc.)
prices skyrocketed as a result, hitting the poorest segments of the

about 5000 CFA francs in 1972. Getting the bottled gas required a 1,500 francs CFA deposit and an additional 1,250 francs CFA for the gas. A 12.5kg jar of gas is usually common and would last about four to six weeks with regular cooking for two persons. While it could turn out to be cheaper than kerosine in the long run, the initial expense involved was quite prohibitive considering the income levels. The average monthly income was about 20,000 CFA francs but there were the rents to pay (on the average about 3,000 francs CFA), the electricity bills for those that had it, and the family responsibilities resulting from the extended family system even for those who were single. Needless to say, gas, no matter how convenient and how popular, was out of reach of the urban and rural poor. By June of 1977, the price of the same 12.5 kg jar of gas had more than doubled to 3000 francs CFA and so had the deposit and the cost of the stove. About 10 to 15 percent of the urban population use bottled gas for cooking.

Kerosine stoves are a slightly different matter. Such stoves are much cheaper than the gas stoves. A kerosine stove with a double burner in 1972 cost about 800 to 1,000 CFA francs and kerosine about 28 francs a litre. Between 1973 and 1975, the price of kerosine rose steadily and by December of 1976 was about 40 francs CFA per litre even though it is most likely being subsidized. In the long run, it could not be safely said that kerosine stoves were cheaper to operate, and they are definitely slower cookers and less efficient. But requiring less of an immediate financial outlay to own and operate, they are much more common than gas stoves with about 25 percent of the urban population using them for cooking. Most kero-sine stoves are used by young people as they feel that such stoves (whether rightly or not) are a step up from the messy and often troublesome firewood or charcoal cooking. In addition, they would rather be seen carrying a can of kerosine or a jar of gas than a bundle of firewood or a sack of charcoal. Here is a question of attitude which has to be reckoned with when the issues of cost of fuels, their availability and alternatives and improved technologies for household consumption of energy are discussed.

Even in urban areas where electricity is available, about 45-50 percent of the population use kerosine lamps for lighting. This seems to represent roughly the proportion of the less well-off segments of the urban population. In urban areas where electricity is not available, as well as in the rural areas, upwards of 98 percent of the population use kerosine lamps for lighting. Kerosine refrigerators are used in areas without electricity and the need for them again arises not because of a desire to preserve food but for other reasons (cold water, drinks). In such areas, bars and hotels that do not have private electricity generators account for the use of most of such refrigerators.

To sum up this section, it could be said that domestic energy consumption of commercial fuels in the country revolves around kerosine (for cooking, lighting and some refrigeration) and bottled gas (cooking only). Where cooking is concerned, the poor of the rural and urban areas are left out of the demand for those fuels because they cannot begin to afford the appliances necessary to use such fuels. Where lighting is concerned, about half the country's urban population and most of the rural consume kerosine.

3. Noncommercial Energy

Domestic demand for noncommercial energy involves mainly two types of fuels--firewood and charcoal--and to a lesser extent a third one--palm kernel oil. It is termed noncommercial because most households (but by no means all) that use those fuels either gather or make their own. Only about

10-20 percent of the people who use wood and/or charcoal buy them. These are all in the urban areas. Animal and human wastes are not sources of energy in Cameroon. Animal wastes, particularly cow dung, are used as manure and as insecticide. The dung is dissolved in water and splashed or sprayed on crops, supposedly providing an effective deterrent against insects. Palm kernel oil, which is oil extracted from the seeds inside an oil palm fruit, is used as fuel for some lighting as well as its usual function of rubbing oil.

Firewood and charcoal are used almost always for cooking, ironing, drying and smoking meats (preservation), some space heating, and drying grains to be planted during the planting season. Except for a few houses owned by wealthy absentee owners (these quite often have modern appliances-- gas stoves or electric cookers), all of the households in the rural areas use either firewood or charcoal for their cooking needs. The use of either charcoal or firewood depends in degree on the part of the country. Most of the country is endowed with forests from which an adequate supply of wood could be obtained fairly easily. But wood in some areas does not burn very well, giving off too much smoke, thus causing a need to burn this wood under a mound of earth to obtain charcoal which is less smokey. For an adequate supply of fuelwood therefore, the rural areas face few problems at present. The greatest problems are currently being faced by that segment of the urban population that relies on wood for fuel. The growth of urban centers has resulted or is resulting in a declining of the surrounding forest areas from which wood could be obtained and thus such households now have greater distances to go to gather wood or simply have to purchase firewood or char- coal from the growing number of firewood and charcoal merchants in the cities and towns. In 1977, firewood which used to cost about 1000 francs CFA a stere in 1972 had gone up to 2315 CFA francs and charcoal which cost an average of 19 francs CFA per kilogram in 1972 was averaging 55 CFA francs per Kg in 1977. That is indeed expensive for a country, one of whose greatest natural resources is the forest. The declining forest would not seem to totally explain such sharp increases in price in a short time; otherwise, if that decline was totally responsible, then a very grave situation has obviously developed in the urban areas of the country. Cooking with firewood in about 90 percent of the households that rely on firewood for fuel is done on open fires, usually with three stones placed in a triangular manner to provide a balance for the cooking pot and space for the wood between the stones. The other 11 percent use firewood stoves and this group is usually urban.

When charcoal is used for cooking, a metal basket (locally made), is used in certain cases and in others the triangular stone pattern is employed. For some urban areas, wood stoves are converted into charcoal stoves. No modification is necessary on the stoves except for ensuring that the stove door is closed when it is loaded with charcoal.

Palm kernel oil when used as fuel for lighting is used much the seme way as kerosine. However, it does not work in pressure lamps. It works only in bush lamps. Less than 2 percent of the population, almost all of them rural poor, use palm kernel oil for lighting.

For ironing, in all households in rural areas without electricity and even in some of those with electricity but that cannot afford electric irons, charcoal is used for ironing. Usually charcoal is loaded in a box type metal iron and lit and when the metal gets hot the ironing is done. When the iron gets too hot, the bottom part of it is dipped a number of times

in cold water. In urban areas without electricity and in most of the poor
segments of the urban areas with electricity, this same type of appliance is
used.

One interesting thing worth noting about the use of firewood and/or
charcoal for cooking in Cameroon is that even in the wealthy or more well-
to-do households that have gas stoves, kerosine stoves or electric stoves,
firewood and/or charcoal are still used to a certain extent. This is the
result of traditional beliefs that hold that food cooked with the traditional fuels taste better. People use gas, kerosine or electricity just
because they are more convenient.

As far as agriculture is concerned, little if any irrigation is used in
the country. Most of the country's agriculture is rainfed as a result of
abundant rainfall. Thus, energy use at present for agriculture is only in
the form of human labor for the poor and diesel-run machines for some of the
rich farmers. Direct heat from the sun is used for drying of some crops
like cocoa end coffee both by the poor and the rich farmers.

4. Trends in Energy Use

Increasing urbanization is resulting in a greater reliance on commercial forms of energy which are usually more expensive. The country has
abundant noncommercial resources of fuels, but more efficient appliances
are needed to use this energy better and also make these fuels more
attractive and thereby reduce the dependence on the presently mostly
imported commercial fuel. Oil and gas have been discovered in the country
and some is currently being extracted and refined. This may lead to a
decrease in commercial energy prices at home, but the country can make use

of more foreign exchange by selling most of this fuel abroad. More research thus has to be done on ways to improve noncommercial energy use and make it more attractive. Cameroon has one of the greatest hydroelectric potentials in the world, and if the economics make it feasible, this should be a source that the country could look to in order to satisfy more of its domestic energy needs, thus freeing more petroleum products for export. The initial costs are certainly going to be great but in the long run would prove to be sensible as the need for diesel to run thermal plants would decrease as well as the fact that the often overlooked costs of transporting this fuel would be eliminated.

Other forms of energy outside of those discussed do not presently play an important role, if any at all, in the overall energy situation of the country. However, the potential for these other forms of energy is there if only the will, desire and efforts to harness and develop them are present. These forms are solar, geothermal and biomass.

Finally, though there is a Ministry of Energy in the country, there is no definite energy policy in the country and the country's energy "problems" (skyrocketing prices, depleting resources) can be traced in part to this fact. The Ministry has thus far seemed to occupy itself only with the development of petroleum resources with just about every press release dealing with the petroleum issue only. Even here new questions are raised as nobody is actually sure how much petroleum the country has, and it would seem dangerous to entirely rely on it when the issue is so clouded.

Finally a note on the price increases noted earlier in the text. Below are a table and graph dealing with the evolution of price indices for certain sectors, towns and the economy as a whole. Using 1966 as a base year of 100, prices did not show a steep increase until after 1973/74. Transportation prices showed the steepest increases, followed by food. Prices for energy and fuels which includes kerosine, petrol, charcoal, fuelwood and electricity rose slower than all other prices according to the price indices. These price indices may not reflect accurately the situation as it is known for a fact that petrol prices for example more than doubled between 1973 and 1974. Whether these steep price increases can all be attributed to the quadrupling of oil prices in 1973/74 is a highly debatable issue. Inflation is another factor whose effect has to be taken into account.

Table B-1. Evolution of Price Indices for Certain Sectors, Towns, and the Economy (1966=100)

						% change	
							1973/74–
						1971/72–	1974/75 &
	71/72	72/73	73/74	74/75	76/77	1973/74	1976/77
Energy and fuels	118	121	128.5	152.6	190	8.90	18.75 47.86
Transport	115.1	117.5	128	205.7	215	11.21	60.70 67.97
General	120.3	126	138	168.5	195	14.71	18.10 41.30
Food (averages) --for the whole country	121	131	144	179	200.1	19.01	24.31 38.96
--for individual towns							
(1) Yaounde	114.3	120.6	136.6	166.6	211	19.51	21.96 & 54.47
(2) Douala	120.9	127.5	135.3	161.2	198	11.91	19.14 & 46.34
(3) Victoria	130.7	145.1	160.1	211.2	N/A	22.49	31.79

Source: Ministry of Economic Development and Planning, Directorate of Statistics and National Accounts, Bulletin Mensuel de Statistique, 1965/66--1976/77 and June 1977.

Appendix C

ENERGY CONSUMPTION DEFINITIONS AND ESTIMATES

The focus of this study is the direct use of energy by poor households, that is, energy consumed for household tasks such as cooking,
heating, cooling, ironing and water heating. In principle, that part of
energy consumption in "productive" activities is excluded.

Household energy consumption so defined is relatively easy to identify
in industrialized countries where household activities are for the
most part clearly distinct from activities of a commercial nature. In developing countries, however, it is rather more difficult to draw this
distinction. In rural areas, household consumption may include energy
inputs into "productive" agricultural activities, and in towns, household
energy consumption might include some consumption related to commercial
activities such as electricity used in professional activities (such as the
operation of power tools used in bicycles or car repair shops).

We do not include the energy embodied in the whole range of other goods
and services purchased by households, though an exception might be
made for energy embodied in transport. Among the rural poor commercial
energy embodied in transport is minimal. On the other hand, the urban poor
are heavy users of public transport for journeys to and from work. As
transport has a high energy content, and as transport patterns are amenable
to change in rapidly growing urban areas, we make some sporadic attempt to
include it.

These distinctions are not tidy either in concept or in practice. In principle, however, we are trying to establish data on (a) energy consumption by the rural poor in food preparation and household operations, and (b) for the urban poor, energy consumption in household operations (including probably handicrafts and small-scale industrial activities) and transport. In addition, unless otherwise specified, energy consumption and supply include both commercial and noncommercial fuels, but exclude metabolic or animate energy.

Energy Consumption Estimates

Table C-1 which underpins table II-1 in the body of the text, gives details of sources, conversion factors, and other relevant information required to make estimates of fuelwood consumption. It will be appreciated from this table that the construction of comparable estimates among countries is a complex undertaking, and the results must be interpreted with every caution.

Note: The conversion of wood and the non-commercial fuels mentioned in the footnote to the table was made at the following rates:

Kenya, Lebanon, Sudan

Tanzania, Thailand,

Uganda, and Nepal

    Wood $1\ m^3 = 9.67$ GJ

Bangladesh

    Wood and twigs   1 tonne = 13 GJ

    Dung   1 tonne = 9 GJ

    Vegetable waste   1 tonne = 12 GJ

India

    Wood   1 tonne = 15 GJ

    Dung   1 tonne = 17 GJ

    Crop wastes   1 tonne = 12 GJ

Upper Volta

    Wood   1 tonne = 13 GJ

    Crop wastes   1 tonne = 12 GJ

Table C-1. Household Fuelwood Usage (with notes on other traditional fuel usage)

Country	Year	Population	Charcoal (percent)	Reference conversion	Original amounts and units	Tons per capita	GJ (10^9 joules) per capita
Gambia	1973	Rural Town (25%)	9 54	[ODA survey] Arnold, 1978, tables 3 & 4	1.32 m^3 per capita " 1.44 "	0.96 1.0	13 14
India	1970	--	--	[Nat'l. Comm. Agric.] Arnold, 1978, tables 3 & 4	0.38 "	0.27	3.7
Kenya	1960	--	6	Arnold, 1978, tables 3 & 4 [assume 9.67 GJ/m^3]	0.98 "	0.71	9.5
Lebanon	1959–1963	Urban (20%)	37	[FAO surveys] Arnold, 1978, tables 3 & 4	0.17 "	0.12	1.6
Sudan	1962	Urban (15%)	42	[FAO surveys] Arnold, 1978, tables 3 & 4	1.63 "	1.2	16
Tanzania	1960–1961 1968–1969	Urban (3%) Rural Town City	-- 1 28 77	[FAO surveys] Arnold, 1978, tables 3 & 4	1.12 " 2.18 " 1.59 " 0.81 "	0.81 1.6 1.1 0.58	11 21 15 7.8
Thailand	1970	Rural Town City	40 88 90	Arnold, 1978, tables 3 & 4	1.27 " 1.00 " 1.00 "	0.91 0.72 0.72	12 9.7 9.7
Uganda	1959			Arnold, 1978 tables 3 & 4	1.41 "		14

(continued)

Table C-1. Household Fuelwood Usage (cont.)

151

Country	Year	Population	Charcoal (percent)	Reference conversion	Original amounts and units	Tons per capita	GJ (10^9 joules) per capita
Bangladesh[1]	1973(?)	Assume 77M population	--	Bangladesh-1976, tables 1.2+, pp. 3-92 [13 GJ/t, wood & twigs]	2 million (long) tons [wood & twigs]	--	0.34
India[2]	1964(?)	Rural	--	Henderson, 1975	126 million tons	--	4.3
India[3]	early 1960s	Assume 400 M population	--	ESIC	120 " "	0.30	4.5
Bangladesh	1976	Assume 77 M population	--	Bangladesh, 1976, App. I, Part 5, pp. 5-32ff, Special Sample Survey	2.2 million tons [rural]	--	0.37
India[4]	1970-1971	Assume 550 M population	--	[domestic] Fuel Plan, 1972 [NCAER, Energy Survey Committee, p. 297]	$116.62 \ 10^6$ tons coal replacement	--	6.1
Upper Volta[5] (Ranga, Boulenga)	?	--	--	Ernst, 1977 (2 villages)	1.49 kg. daily	0.31-0.54	4.0, 7.0
Nepal[6]	?	--	--	Nepal, 1976, table 2.2	--	0.546	7.1
Nepal	1970, 1971, 1972, 1973, variously	--	--	[Earl, 1975] Clark, 1970 Sinden, 1971 Butkas, 1972	0.20 m^3 per capita 2.55 " " 1.09, 1.49, 1.34 m^3	-- --	1.9 25 10, 14, 13
				Earl, 1973	0.85, 0.95, 0.52 m^3 per capita		8.2, 9.2, 5.0
				FAO, 1970 [assume 9.67 GJ/m^3]	0.57 m^3 per capita	--	5.5

(continued)

Table C-1. Household Fuelwood Usage (cont.)

Country	Year	Remarks	Charcoal (percent)	Reference conversion	Original amounts and units	Tons per capita	GJ (10^9 joules) per capita
Nigeria (Batagawara, 1,400 population)		Note: 1-1.5 tons per capita for wood apparently assumed	--	Makhijani & Poole, 1975	21 10^9 Btu		16
Tanzania (Kilombero, 100 population, cool nights)			--	Makhijani & Poole, 1975	2.2 10^9 Btu		23
Bolivia (Quebreda, 6 population, cold)		Apparently 2 tons assumed for U.S. 3 tons	--	Makhijani & Poole, 1975, tables 2-15, 12, 21, 18, 4	0.2 10^9 Btu		35
Mexico (Arango, 420 population, arid subtropics)		Assume electricity, gas usage		Makhijani & Poole, 1975	6 10^9 Btu (wood resid.)		15 (incl. resid.)
India (Mangaon, 1,000 population)				Makhijani & Poole, 1975	1 10^9 Btu		1

[1] Other consumption estimated (in GJ per capita) at 1.3 dung, 1.2 vegetable wastes, 0.20 commercial.

[2] Other consumption estimated (in GJ per capita) at 2.2 dung and 1.4 coke.

[3] Other consumption estimated (in GJ per capita) at 2.0 dung and 0.9 vegetable wastes.

[4] Other consumption estimated (in GJ per capita) at 1.4 dung, 1.9 vegetable wastes, 0.21 coal, 1.4 oil, 0.2 electric.

[5] Consumption of wastes estimated at 3.5 GJ per capita.

[6] Other consumption estimated (in GJ per capita) at 0.46 dung and 0.9 vegetable wastes.